Environment and Society

Environment and Society

Ghanshyam Kushwaha

GenNext Publication

ISBN: 978-93-5324-939-7 (HB)

"An Imprint of Kalpaz Publication"

First Published, 2022

Published by

GenNext Publication
5, Ansari Road
Daryaganj, New Delhi-110002
Phone: 011-47034999, 9811692060
E-mail: gennextpublication@hotmail.com

Printed at: Gyan Press, Delhi.

Dedicated

to

Maa & Babuji

Contents

Preface

Relation of mankind with its environment is a bilateral phenomenon since time immemorial. Cradles of nature had been nurturing human beings, but due to certain unfriendly measures undertaken by society as a whole this equilibrium received a setback. So, it became a long-time commitment to preserve nature. The Year 2020 tipped open a global pouring of change exposing some environmental issues all over the world. Now-a-days we are poised with a paradigm shift but in its essence, this is beyond local issues. As nature is not confined with in man-made geographical boundaries of countries, so common cause aroused common concerns. Old saying 'World is too much with us' seems true with reference to environment. During a very long course of time we were pressed hard to study environmental issues in all the branches of study including Geography, Geology, Zoology, Botany, Sociology and Economics etc. It became highly interesting and useful subject. It would not be a hyperbole in claiming it as a penchant in anyone's life.

This book explores different dimensions and aspects of the environment including man-environment relations, environmental pollution, protection, conservation, planning, promotion and attempts made at national and international level. This book aims at to provide thorough idea of different aspects of man - environment relations. My efforts are here to meet the demands of students and fellow teachers. This book will also bring some glimpses of burning contemporary issues like acid rain, drinkable water scarcity, climate change and global warming. I hope this book will certainly cater the needs and expectations of the readers as it has been updated with recent facts and data.

Your valuable comments and reviews will make me prosperous and able to update the book in forthcoming editions.

With best wishes.

Acknowledgement

I place on record my heartfelt gratitude to all those who have motivated and supported me to complete this book. I am extremely grateful to my teachers for their intellectual support, encouragement and criticism in both certain and uncertain moments. It promoted me to complete this work in time. I am highly obliged to take the opportunity to express my sincere thanks to all esteemed faculty members of my college for their unconditional love and logistic support that proved instrumental for me. Their support boosted my self-confidence to accomplish this venture. My sincere thanks to all of them. Above all, I am highly obliged to my parents, whom I am greatly indebted as they have brought me up with warm love and passion. Their debt upon me is beyond expression.

My wife Dr. Sangita has always been a good adviser and motivator. Her suggestions boosted my morale to complete this book in time. I remember my son Abhinav for his fascinating love and affection during this work. I also express my hearty gratitude to all my friends from different universities and colleges for always encouraging me, reassuring me of my potential that I often failed to see. Their unconditional support and help made me thoughtful.

Last but not the least, I also want to express my thanks to publisher of the book. My heart is full of thanks to all favoures that I have received from every person in this academic journey.

I feel overwhelmed with pleasure while handing over this book to you all.

Thanks.

Introduction

We are consuming natural resources at a rate much higher than that at which nature can regenerate them. We are polluting the environment at a rate greater than its ability to absorb the pollution. Thus, it is an unsustainable way of living and it can only lead to environmental problems.

Environment is the greatest gift of nature to man. It is a constituent of a-biotic (Non-count) components like air, water, light etc. and biotic living components like plants, animals, human beings etc. which are responsible for the survival and continuance of life on this earth. Everything that surrounds us like, air, water, land, animals and mountains come under environment. It can be divided into the physical, chemical and biological environment. The physical environment is air, ground and water. Acid, gases and other compounds make the chemical component of nature. The biological component comprises plants, animals and bacteria. Environment can also be divided into man-made and natural. The natural environment comprises oceans, rivers, forests, deserts and air. The man-made environment consists of agricultural fields, urban centers, industries, SEZs markets and other facets.

Thus, environment can be called a system from which we obtain resources like water, food and shelter etc. Naturally, the available natural resources are water, trees, minerals and hydro-electric power. We depend on the environment to live. But to fulfill our needs, for achieving development and prosperity and for meeting the demands of the rapid increase of population we are polluting and depleting the environment. The emission of gases from factories and vehicles fill the air with poisonous gases. Excessive use of chemical fertilisers and harmful insecticides, pesticides for the growth of plants has led the damaging of the qualities of soils. The development of industries and use of oil and fuels are depleting our renewable natural resources.

Environment is a very broad concept. The term 'environment' originates from the French words 'environ' or 'environner' meaning 'around', 'round-about', 'to surround' or 'to encompass'. The environment is both physical and biological concept, it includes both the non-living (a-biotic) and living (biotic) components of the planet earth. In order to understand environment, it is essential to understand "Environment Chemistry" i.e. the chemical constituents of the environment. Environment chemistry thus is a science of chemical changes occurring in the environment. The Earth's environment constitutes about 78.09 percent nitrogen, 20.95 percent oxygen, and 0.93 percent argon. Apart from this 0.03 percent including the greenhouse gases like carbon dioxide, methane, nitrous oxide and ozone. The environmental study is the understanding of sources, reactions, transport, efforts and fates of chemical species in the water, soil and air environment and the effect of human activities upon environmental segments such as atmosphere, hydrosphere, lithosphere and biosphere.

Environment

The main and the foremost aim of an environmentalist is to study the nature as well quantify the pollutants in the environment. Hence environmentalists find it difficult to define "Environment" in few lines. In fact, the term environment is a composite term used for the conditions in which organisms live and thus composes of the air, water, food and sunlight. According to some philosopher's environment has been defined in a number of ways:

Environment is the sum of all social, economical, biological, physical or chemical factors which constitute the surroundings of man, who is both creator and molder of his environment.

OR,

Environment is referred to the sum total of natural conditions, which surround us at a given point and space in time.

OR,

Environment represents the physical component of the earth of which man is an important factor who influences his environment.

OR,

Environment is a total complex view of the world as it functions at any time, with a multitude of special elements and socio-economic systems which are distinguished by quality and attributes of space and mode of behaviour of biotic and a-biotic forms of lives.

Thus, environment is the surroundings in which living and non-living things live, interact, grow and perish. The conditions present in the surroundings govern the life of creatures therein. The four major components of environment include lithosphere, hydrosphere, atmosphere and biosphere, corresponding to rocks, water, air and life respectively. There is continuous interaction among these four zones. These interactions involve the transport of various elements, compounds and energy forms. These zones are explained as follows. [Fig. 1 (A). 1]

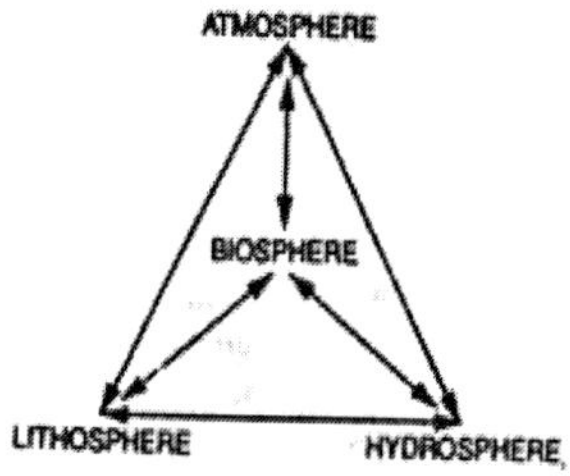

(Fig. 1(A).1)
Interaction of environmental components

Lithosphere is the outermost layer of earth called crust, which is made of different minerals. Its depth can reach up to 100 kilometers and is found on both land (terrestrial crust) and oceans (oceanic crust). The main component of lithosphere is earth's tectonic plates which are seven major and twenty minors in numbers. Basically, lithosphere is nothing but a crustal system composed of various layers: Core, mantle and outer crust. Various elements constitute such crustal layer in mixture of different proportions. In general, the earth curst is composed of three major classes of rocks (as classified on the basis of their mode of origin): Igneous rocks, sedimentary rocks and metamorphosed rocks. There are two types of crusts – continental crust which is composed of granitic rocks in silicon aluminium and with a mean density of 2.8; the other oceanic crust which is basaltic in composition consisting of more basic minerals and has a mean density of 3.0. Overall, the average density of the earth is 5.5 gm/c.c.

Hydrosphere comprises of all forms of water bodies on earth including oceans, seas, rivers, lakes, ponds, streams etc. It covers 70% of earth's surface. 97.5% of water found on Earth is in the oceans in the form of salt water. Only 2.5 % of water on Earth is freshwater. Out of this, 30.8% is available as groundwater and 68.9% is in frozen forms as in glaciers. Amount of 0.3% is available in rivers, reservoirs and lakes and is easily accessible to man. We use water at home, in industry, in agriculture, and for recreation. These applications differ widely in the quantity and quality of the water that they require. In one way or another we use all available sources- inland waters, ground water, and even oceanic water. The demand for global water resources increasing day-by-day though availability of pure fresh water has been decreasing severely. Thus, there is need to make precious use of pure fresh water and their fruitful storage and conservation.

Atmosphere is gaseous layer enveloping the Earth. The atmosphere with oxygen in abundance is unique to Earth and sustains life. It mainly comprises 78.08% nitrogen, 20.95% oxygen, 0.93% argon, 0.038% carbon dioxide, and traces of hydrogen, helium, and noble gases. The amount of water vapour present is variable.

The gases like Nitrogen, Oxygen, Argon, Carbon dioxide and water vapour etc. together make up the total volume of atmosphere.

Together with suspended particulates, viz. dust and soot constitute the gaseous turbidity particularly in troposphere. However, the composition of atmosphere and so also the structure is variable in time and space.

The vertical structure of atmosphere is very much related to radiant energy absorption. Below 60 km. there are two main zones of absorption at the Earth's surface and in the Ozone layer. The absorbed energy is redistributed by radiation, conduction and convection.

There are, therefore, two temperature maxima: at the Earth's surface and at an elevation of 50 km. above each of these maxima there is mainly convectional mixing. Temperature in these mixing layers decreases with height above the heat source. The lower of

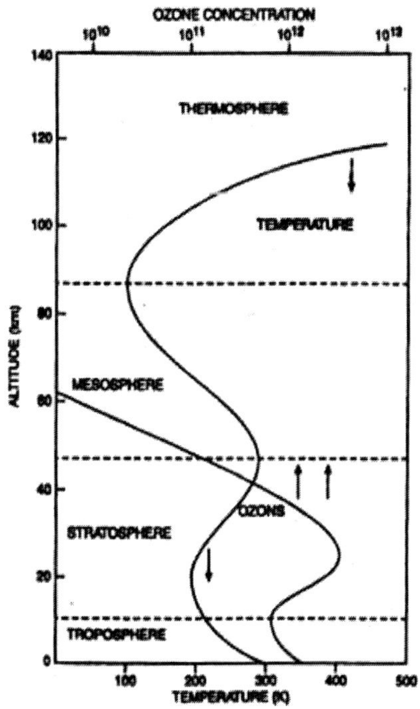

(Fig. 1(A).2)
(Temperature profile of atmospheric layers)

these two zones is referred to as troposphere and the upper is the mesosphere.

These are separated by a layer of little mixing in which the atmosphere tends towards a layered structure referred as the stratosphere. Between the ionosphere and the stratosphere is the tropopause which marks the approximate upper limit of mixing in the lower atmosphere. The average height of this is usually given as 11 km., but this varies over the earth. About 50 percent of the atmosphere lies below the altitude of 5.6 kilometer and 97 percent of the atmosphere is confined to the height of only 29 kilometers.

In tropical latitude its average height is 16 km. and in polar latitude it is only 10 km. There is one further zone of heating, above the mesosphere and more than 90 km. from the Earth's surface where shortwave ultraviolet radiation is absorbed by many oxygen molecules present at this height. This is referred to as thermosphere.

Within this layer, ionisation occurs which produces charged ions and free electrons. Beyond the thermosphere, at a height of approximately 700 km, lies the exosphere where the atmosphere has an extremely low density. At this level there are increasing numbers of ionisation particles which are concentrated into bands referred to as the Van Allen radiation belts.

However, this simple model of vertical structure can be simplified to provide a model of the atmosphere as two concentric shells the boundaries of which are defined by the stratopause at approximately 50 km. above the Earth's surface and a hypothetical outer limit of the atmosphere, at approximately 80,000 km.

Below the stratopause, in the stratosphere and troposphere, there is 99% of the total mass of the atmosphere and it is at this level that atmospheric circulatory systems operate. Beyond the stratopause a layer of nearly 80,000 km. thick contains only 1 % of total atmospheric mass and experiences ionisation by high-energy, short wavelength solar radiation.

Biosphere refers to all the regions on Earth where life exists. It is also called as a life supporting layer which surrounds the earth and makes plant and animal life possible without any protective device. The ecosystems that support life could be in soil, air, water or land. The term Biosphere was coined by Geologist Edward Suess who used this term for place on Earth where life can be found. Biosphere refers to the sum total of all living matter, the biomass or biota. It extends from the polar ice caps to the equator, with each region harbouring some life form suitable to the conditions there. Within the biosphere, there are several major regions containing specific types of ecosystems. These major regions are called biomes. Biomes are then recognised by the types of dominant ecosystem- tropical rainforests, temperate forests, prairies, deserts, and arctic tundra.

The average thickness of the biosphere or life supporting layer consisting of air, water, soil and rock is about 30 kilometers. The upper limit of the biosphere is determined by the availability of oxygen, moisture, temperature and air pressure. Decrease in oxygen, moisture, temperature and air pressure with increase in height in the atmosphere limits the upper boundary of the atmosphere.

Thus, everything that affects human lives is collectively known as environment. As human beings we are concerned for our surrounding conditions that affect people and other organisms. Environment is not of static existence and it changes from time to time and place to place, sometimes gradually or else vigorously. Men as well as other organisms are equally influenced by these changes. The sudden environmental changes may not suit all the creatures. Those who could not adapt these variations vanished/ disappeared with time, the giant dinosaur's extinction is an example.

Today, everywhere in the world there is growing concern about the deteriorating quality of environmental lives and efforts are being made to stop the misuse of widespread environment and improve its quality. The first worldwide meeting of heads of state in response to the concerns for the environment took place at the Earth Summit, which is also known as the United Nations Conference on Environment and Development (UNCED) in Rio de Janeiro in 1992. This summit reflects world-wide concern about the deteriorating quality of our natural environment. International Environment Education Programme is another outcome of the summit 1992 and efforts are being made globally to educate people at each level of society about the environmental problems. The recent UN Climate Change Conference COP-25 (2-13 December 2019) took place under the presidency of the government of Chile which objectives was to complete several matters with respect to the full operationalisation of the Paris Climate Change Agreement. More than five years after the Paris Agreement was concluded, there is no consensus on raising ambition to reduce emissions, making access to low carbon technologies easier, and adequately funding mitigation and adaptation.

COVID-19 had the unexpected effect of marginally and temporarily depressing emissions. The IPCC's analysis depicts the collapse of climate systems at large scale. Heatwaves and heavy rainfall events experienced with increasing frequency and intensity are just two of these, while disruptions to the global water cycle pose a more unpredictable threat. Also, if emissions continue to rise, oceans and land, two important sinks and the latter a key part of India's climate action plan, would be greatly weakened in their ability to absorb atmospheric carbon dioxide. The new report sets the stage for the COP26 conference in November. The only one course to adopt there is for developed countries with legacy emissions to effect deep cuts, transfer technology without strings to emerging economies and heavily fund mitigation and adaptation. Developing nations should then have no hesitation in committing themselves to steeper emissions cuts.

The environment in which we live and work, affects our thinking, feelings, and behaviours. The relationship between man and environment is, however, reciprocal. That is, human beings are affected by the environment and they affect the environment as well. The human-environment interaction has five major components. These components are briefly described below:

1. *Physical Environment:* It includes aspects of natural environment such as climate, terrain, temperature, rainfall, flora and fauna, etc.
2. *Social-cultural Environment:* It includes all aspects of cultural environment such as norms, values, customs and socialisation of individuals in the society etc. It includes all the aspects dealing with human beings and their creations.

3. *Environmental Orientations:* It refers to the beliefs that people hold about their environment. For example, some people who believe and held the view that environment is equivalent to God. They perceive all its aspects with respect and preserve the natural attributes and try to maintain it in a perfect form and do not degrade it.
4. *Environmental Behaviour:* It refers to the use of natural environment by the human beings in the course of social interactions. For example, considering the environment as personal space, where the individual identifies himself with environment.
5. *Products of Behaviour:* These include the outcomes of people's actions such as homes, cities, dams, schools, etc. That is, these are products or outcomes dealing with the environment.

All the above aspects of environment depict the important constituents of the study of interaction between environment and the human beings. It is very important to understand that human beings are part of the environment and degradation of environment will result in extinction of human being and also the other forms of life. Therefore, it is the sole responsibility of every individual to maintain the environment in trim condition, its destruction means destruction of human life.

Chapter - 1

Man–Environment Relationship

The relationship between man and environment is most intimate. Man adopted some activities to sustain himself on the earth from his birth. Man is a social animal and that he loves to live in society with other human beings, is a general conception about his basic behavioural pattern. But the fact remains that without a social environment, no stability would be brought to his status as an individual.

According to one of the popular and widely accepted definitions, human geography is the study of "man and his adjustment to his natural environment". There are various racial and ethnic groups in the world and the geo-climatic conditions of the many parts of the earth also differ from each other substantially. Each society or ethnic group uses, misuses and under-uses its natural environmental resource base according to its cultural demand and technological advancement. For example, the mode of life of Pygmies of Congo basin differs from that of the Badawins of Saudi Arabia. Likewise, the Aboriginals of Australian desert and Eskimos of Tundra region have been compelled by their environments to practice hunting for their survival. The Nagas, who used to practice head-hunting till recent past, have very closed territorial demarcation and their lifestyle and cultural practices which is altogether different from the Nepalese and Kukis living in the same environment. The Gujjars and Bakarwals, who oscillate in the higher Himalayas and the Shiwaliks in the summer and winter seasons, differ from the Kashmiris and Dogras who live in the same habitat. Thus, these variations in their respective lifestyles are the expressions of man's adjustment to his natural environment.

The impact of environment on man and his adaptation to physical environment have been emphasized by the Greek, Roman and Arab scholars. Aristotle and Darwin were also of the same view that man struggles for his survival.

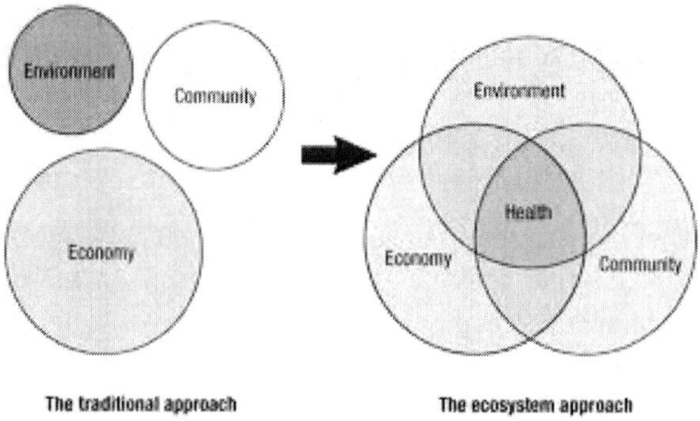

Apart from material gains and cultural achievements, food, clothing, shelter, tools, technology, customs, traditions, socio-economic institutions, higher needs like religion, faith, language, literature, fine arts and folklore, folk medicine etc., are directly or indirectly influenced by the physical environment. In other words, man has molded his habits and lifestyle according to his physical surroundings and natural endowments.

The impact of man on environment is also a topic of growing importance in human geography. The adjustment of man to his physical environment in typical geographical regions like equatorial, hot deserts and tundra is of great relevance to human geography as it helps in understanding the symbolic relationship between social groups and their natural environment.

Geography is a broad subject with great variation. It seeks to explain the relationships between man and his environment through studies both thematic and regional, at a number of scales. In doing this, Geography provides an opportunity to satisfy a person's curiosity as to why things are the way they are, who he/she is, and what the relationship between them is. To complete a recognisable Geographical study, a number of methods may be used however definite skills are required. These skills include data collection, analysis, interpretation and generalisation of information at both levels, i.e., statistical and graphical. The subject promotes a greater awareness of the world as a physical entity and a human habitat and gives meaning to this awareness. It is at once, full of information of intrinsic value and concepts and skills of extrinsic value. No child's education can be complete without an awareness of Geography. The subject serves to open the mind to the greatness and beauty of the world, but also to the inevitable fact that it is finite, with finite resources and in danger through the activities of man, and of threatening to the extinction of all life. Every individual, especially in these days of depleting Ozone, Greenhouse gases, social inequality and discrimination, and faulty land use planning, should be educated to try and create a more harmonious way for Man to live with nature environment. We may refer this as sustainable living.

Fig. Man and Environment Relationship.

The relationship between human beings and surrounding environment has varied from nomadic life to the settled one and also to the present era of humans living. The relationship between natural environment and human beings has also been changing from place to place at any given period of time. For example, early humans considered the environment to be dominant. In the early time of human's interaction with natural environment they were afraid of lightning and thunder, dense forests, wild animals, droughts and floods, vast oceans and large rivers etc. The environment has considerably affected human beings right from his evolution. The environment affects humans in many ways. Population on the earth varies due to variation in the environment.

The main factors which affect the distribution of population and human settlement are:

- **Relief of Land:** The populations in the high mountainous areas, such as the Himalayas and in deserted areas like Thar of Rajasthan in India, Andes in South America, Rocky in North America, etc., have very low population settlement level. This is because the relief is rugged here which represents major obstacles in the construction of roads, railways and communication. Due to steep slopes, agricultural activities are difficult and industries also could not be well developed. These areas very less economic value and less population and hence have small isolated human settlements. Whereas the plain areas of the world are most suitable for human settlement. On the other side, fertile plains of Gangetic region in India, Indus in Pakistan, Hwang-Ho in China and plains of Europe have dense population settlement with compact or huge semi-compact type of settlement.
- **Climate:** Most of the areas of the earth have population density of less than two persons/sq. km which is not favourable for settlement because of their unfavourable climate. The areas of cold climate like, North Siberia, North Canada, Alaska etc., have low population density. Hot and arid regions of- Sahara, Kalahari Desert in Africa, Great Australian Desert etc. are not suitable for human settlement. In tropical regions due to heavy rain and temperature, the density of population is very low, example in Amazon basin population density is less than two persons/sq. km. But places with favourable climate and favourable terrain, have dense population and hence have compact settlement.

- **Soils:** Fertile alluvial soils encourage dense population which in turn gives rise to compact type of settlement. This is so because alluvial soils give rise to agricultural activities. Likewise, the Java Islands of Indonesia has fertile soil of newly volcanic erupted material and agriculture is an important activity, hence these areas have dense and compact settlements. Whereas in Sumatra, due to infertile soil, the population density is very low.
- **Mineral Deposits:** Mineral wealth is another important factor responsible for population distribution and density. For example, the presence of coal and iron-ore in different parts of the world has attracted dense population settlement over that particular region. Coal mining regions have become regions of dense population for example, Jharkhand in India and gold mines in Australian desert etc.
- **Water supply:** Population distribution is very much affected by water supply. The earliest settlements or civilisations developed on the banks of major rivers, example-Nile, Indus, etc. However, the adequate supply of water provides irrigation facilities to farmers and hence population increases due to increase in primary activities. In dry regions, population is concentrated in those areas where there is water, hence nucleated- circular settlements are found. Thus, it can be said that the environment plays an important role in deciding population distribution, density, settlement type and pattern. The Industrial Revolution which provided mechanical power, invention of steam engine and other machinery, greater use of metals etc. gave them opportunities to modify the environment. At the same time agriculture provided abundant food so that they could settle down permanently. The family grew in size and people migrated to different parts, via rail, road and sea, because of improvement in transport system, example the new lands in America and Australia were settled by people from Europe. However, there is another development which enabled humans to survive was the use of preventive and cumulative efforts taken to protect them

from epidemics and diseases. It also increased the span of human life and reduced human death rate. With increase in the knowledge and growing skill and development of human economy, there was a gradual increase in carbon dioxide in the atmosphere. However, it is estimated that concentration of carbon dioxide in the atmosphere is currently at nearly 412 parts per million (ppm) and rising. This represents a 47 percent since the beginning of the Industrial age, when the concentration was near 280 ppm, and an 11 percent increase since 2000, when it was near 370 ppm. (reference: NASA GLOBAL CLIMATE CHANGE, October 9, 2019). Estimation has also revealed the concentration of carbon dioxide increased by 25% in last 100 yrs and the global temperatures have risen from 0.3 degree Celsius to 0.7 degree Celsius. Increase in carbon dioxide is attributed to large scale deforestation and will lead to increase in sea level causing submergence of coastal regions. Burning of coal, oil and petroleum add sulphur dioxide to the atmosphere. Lead, carbon monoxide and nitrogen dioxide are added to the atmosphere from automobile exhaust. These gases result in acid rain which affects aquatic life, example of acid rain in industrial regions of Europe and North America (reference: www.thecanadianencyclopedia.com). Even now substances which were not present previously, are now introduced into the air, water and soils, and the most dangerous one is radioactive substance that spewed into the atmosphere by nuclear explosions. They have adverse effects on all living organisms including human beings and cause death, impairment of limbs, diseases and psychological disorders. The incidence of catastrophe of nuclear disaster at Chernobyl in Ukraine (1988) is a recent example of adverse environmental effects of use of minerals like uranium, thorium etc., through most advanced and sophisticated technology. The environment has already been degraded to such an extent in certain areas that people are forced to migrate. They are facing scarcity of resources like food and energy.

Man's impact on environment has resulted in environmental pollution which not only affects air, water and land but also all organisms of atmosphere. The main points of the impact of man on environment are:

- **Air pollution**- burning of fossil fuels like, coal, petroleum in large quantities from industries to jet aircrafts has resulted in severe air pollution. CFCs are used in aerosol spray cans, refrigerators and farm blowing are responsible for depletion of ozone to 3-4% in last 100 years. As per the World Health Organisation (WHO), exposure to outdoor air pollution contributes to as much as 0.6 to 1.4 percent of the burden of disease and 4.2 million deaths every year.
- **Water pollution**- the major cause of water pollution is the leakage of petroleum oil from ships and oil tankers into the sea and ocean, causes oil slicks which spread rapidly over water and cause severe disaster to marine life and to human depending on marine resources. For example, the leakage of 100000 tonnes of crude oil near Spanish coast in 1976, and leakage of crude oil off Alaskan coast in 1989, off Galicia Spain in 2002 and around Mauritius in July 2020 are a few examples of the many such incidents which tell the story of impact of negligence and failure of technology on environment. The most widespread source of water pollution is disposal of sewage of urban centers into rivers. The Ganga and Yamuna are polluted in this way and the same rivers provide domestic water supply as well. Though the Indian government has approved 'Namami Gange Programme' as 'flagship Programme' to accomplish the twin objectives of effective abatement of pollution, conservation and rejuvenation of National River Ganga. Still the situation of the Rivers is worst. Ocean waters are mostly polluted by discharge of sewage from cities located along the coast.
- **Land degradation**: land degradation is defined as a negative trend in land condition, caused by direct or indirect human-induced processes including anthropogenic climate change, expressed as long-term reduction or loss of at least one of

the following: biological productivity, ecological integrity, or value to humans. Forest degradation is land degradation that occurs in forest land. Deforestation is the conversion of forest to non-forest land and can result in land degradation. It is generally because of dumping of urban solid waste and waste materials from mining centers renders the land unsuitable for further any use. Surface run-off water from such areas pollutes streams and ground water seepage. Saline encrustation of irrigated lands is another form of land degradation. In the region of semi-arid areas, wind action causes deposition of sand on a large scale over cultivated land and rendering it unfit for cultivation. This marks the beginning of desertification. Land degradation is one of the world's most pressing environmental problems and it will worsen without rapid remedial action. Globally, about 25 percent of the total land area has been degraded. When land is degraded, soil carbon and nitrous oxide is released into the atmosphere, making land degradation one of the most important contributors to climate change. Scientists recently warned that 24 billion tonnes of fertile soil was being lost per year, largely due to unsustainable agriculture practices. If this trend continues, 95 percent of the Earth's land areas could become degraded by 2050. Land degradation can be avoided, reduced or reversed by implementing sustainable land management, restoration and rehabilitation practices that simultaneously provide many co-benefits, including adaptation to and mitigation of climate change.

- **Depletion of resources**- with the increasing pressure of population growth in the recent past has consequences into rapid depletion of all kinds of resources. The most striking example of such depletion of resources is the food deficit faced by about almost 100 countries of the world. Forest and land resources are getting severely depleted at a fast rate owing to population pressure. Tropical forests are depleting annually at a rate of 2 per cent. It is estimated that the world is losing 7 percent of top soil per decade. It is obvious that depletion of resources is most significant in respect of non-renewable mineral and power resources. Today, the world is facing severe energy crisis as existing oil and mineral resources may last for a few decades. However, coal reserves are adequate for a few centuries but it cannot replace mineral oil, especially for transport. Humans have now come to realise that their increasing economic activities are threatening their survival on earth. Their survival depends on their realisation that they have to live in coordination with the various elements of natural environment which are properly interconnected. An understanding of the components and processes which take place in environment, the relationship between biotic and a-biotic components, and the assessment of resources with reference to need of people in a region is essential for their survival.

Deterministic Approach

The environmental determinism approach emphasises that landscapes are mainly determined and shaped by the environment. Thus, there can be no exercise of free will on the part of human beings. Here, nature plays an important role in the creation of a landscape. Nature determined the environment and by doing this, nature also influences the way individuals act. The environment thus allows only the strongest to survive. This goes for nature as well as for humans, and is based on the 'survival of the fittest' by Darwin.

Determinism is also a doctrine which stubbornly postulates that all events and phenomenon are the inevitable result of antecedent conditions and that the human beings, in act of apparent choices are the mechanical expression of their hereditary and past environment. Determinism emphasizes the dominant influence of physical forces in shaping man's characteristics and his modes of thought and life. According to this view, the mode of life of different people is enforced upon them by the character of their habitat. Nature determines the kind of work and the mode of life of any individual. Man is given only a passive role.

The ancient Greeks theorised and authored the first formal expressions of environmental determinism that are clearly part of geography's own scholarly past productions. The Greeks had well-developed ideas about the relation between climate, hydrology, vegetation, soil, relief features, and local to global locations and their controls or influences on individual behaviour as well as on collective cultural attributes, attitudes, and actions. Climatic conditions in particular were linked to psycho-physiological states of well-being or malady. In turn, from Hippocrates (500 BC) onward, the doctrine of the four humors i.e., blood, phlegm, yellow and black-biles are held that body balances and imbalances, and hence health itself, were determined mainly by environmental factors. The Hippocratic treatise airs, waters and places served as one of the important bases of Western medical theory for the next two millennia or more. Implicitly, it has also served as a fountainhead of environmentalist thought for an equal duration. However, many Greek philosophers and scholars have expressed elements of this psycho-physiological body of thought, virtually all of them subscribed to the notion that environmental factors influenced the lives and ways of different people and their respective cultures. Herodotus's ethnographic and historical observations on people from different regions and cultures through the ancient ecumene or inhabited world are encyclopedic and offer many instances of environmental-cultural influences. Aristotle is perhaps the most important proponent of climate plus location equaling potential for fruition of civilisation. He was of the opinion that people of cold regions, particularly Europe, were spirited and freedom loving but lacked skill and intelligence.

However, people of hot regions, particularly from Asia, lacked spirit but had skills and intelligence despite their tendencies toward subjection and despotism. Greeks occupied the intermediate climatic and location regimes which were most suited to achieve the golden mean. Aristotle and other philosophers commented in detail on particular and specific environmental effects such as the insalubrities of marshes, the qualities of various kinds of winds, and alluvial soils versus stony soils. In addition to specific local or regional environmental effects, the Greeks conceptualised global controls by latitudinal zones. Aristotle propounded that the torrid-zone, or the lands closest to the equator, were uninhabitable and that those most distant, the frigid-zones, were equally uninhabitable by human beings. Thus, the lands between these extremes, the temperate zone, were the only ones suited for human habitation. Within the temperate zone, the Mediterranean littorals were ideally situated. Most Greek thinkers, and later the Romans, agreed with Aristotle on his appraisal of the temperate latitudes as being most suited for the perfection of human habitation and civilisation.

From the fall of Rome (ca. 500 AD), through the European Middle Ages (500–1500 AD), and on into the Renaissance (ca. 1500–1650 AD), environmentalist doctrines at both the body-physiological and regional-location scales were staples of geographic thought and theory. Afro-Asiatic traditions of geographic thought and practice also embodied environmental determinist concepts and outlooks. During the middle Ages, Muslim scholars like, Ibn Khaldun (1332-1406) accepted most of the environmentalist theory of Greco–Roman antiquity but also inflected their own compendious description of geographies with environmentalist observations. Feng Shui's Chinese philosophy guides the placing of buildings in relation to environmental features, also reflects environmentalist currents within Chinese geographic practice during this period as well as before and subsequently. Medieval Christian scholars such as Thomas Aquinas and Albertus Magnus gave detailed attention to environmentalist explanations of human behaviour according to geographic features and location.

With the onset of the Age of Discovery and the Renaissance (ca. 1500-1650 AD), encounters with new lands and new and rediscovered ideas created new contexts for environmental determinist thought. French political philosopher Jean Bodin (1530-1596) was the main environmental theorist of this period. He drew mostly on Greco-Roman environmentalist theory but modified it with the flood of new geographic knowledge that inundated Europe during the period of 16th century. His main conceptions of both history and politics as determined by geographical factors, mainly climate, laid the foundations for important expressions of environmentalism during the Enlightenment era (1650-1800 AD).

The Enlightenment, or the "Age of Reason," was also an important point of environmental determinist theories. Charles de Second at Baron de Montesquieu (1689–1755) was the most influential and celebrated of these theorists. His, "The Spirit of Laws (1748)" offered a universal treatise on politics and politics of governance. Its elaborate arguments are based heavily on environmentalist reasoning and examples. Climatic conditions offer an overarching explanation for cultural and historical differences and customs. Environmental factors like, relief features, soils, and relative locations account for sub-variations and outcomes. Although environmentalists' arguments were voiced by many enlightened figures, including Jean-Jacques Rousseau and Denis Diderot as they were also challenged. Voltaire, David Hume, and Count Buffon all found fault with the doctrines of climatic causation. This debate carried over into the 19th century and formed one of the central axes on which modern geography was constructed. There was no clear separation between the opposing camps until the early 20th century, when the refutation of environmental determinism became one of the central organising principles of several different strands or schools of geography. For example, in the work of geography's modern founders, Alexander von Humboldt and Carl Ritter, one can find both appeals to environmentalists' explanation and counterevidence. Ritter, however, heavily relied on it, whereas, Humboldt resorted to it only occasionally. Towards the end of the 19th century, Friedrich Ratzel attempted to put environmentalist theory at the center of a new and scientific human geography. The first volume of his Anthropogeography made the case for this approach. His training in Zoology and his evolutionary perspective- more neo-Lamarckian than strictly Darwinian- underwrote the concepts he formulated. Chief ideas among these were the ideas of Lebensraum ("living space") and the state-as-organism. Ratzel's followers, particularly Ellen Churchill Semple, popularised these concepts and introduced an explicitly geographic environmentalism to a broad Anglophone audience. Other American geographers, such as Nathaniel Shaler, William Morris Davis, Albert Brigham, and especially Ellsworth Huntington, helped to make environmentalism the main mode of explanation in American geography during the period circa 1890 to 1920. In its strong forms, turn-of-the-century environmental determinism helped ideologically to legitimate social Darwinism, racism, eugenics, colonialism, and other manifestations of the European and North American drive for global supremacy.

Despite Fredrik Ratzel's initial influence, by the 1920s many European geographers found this theory simplistic and argued that this environmentalism wants both substance and relevance. French historians and geographers counter-posed possibilism as a more nuanced understanding of human-environment relations. Carl Sauer was among the first American geographers to subject environmentalism to sharp critique and to reject it as either a theoretical or a methodological programme for geography. By the 1930s, chorology or the regional approach had largely replaced environmentalism as the main focus of academic geography. By the 1950s, environmental determinism in geography had been largely discredited. Variants of what might be interpreted as environmental determinism continued to be advanced under the banner of Soviet Marxist geography into the 1960s. At the same time, scholars in some of geography's cognate disciplines have resuscitated environmental determinism to explain the uneven developmental trajectories of societies in widely differing historical periods, but particularly in modern times. Even today, in many of these appraisals, tropical lands of the world are inherently doomed to play marginal roles and returns compared with those of temperate climates and latitudes.

The significance of the deterministic school of thought is that the history, culture, norms, values, lifestyle and stage of development of a social group, society or nation are exclusively or largely governed by the physical factors like, relief, terrain, climate, drainage, fauna and flora etc. of environment. The determinists consider man as a passive agent of change on which, the environmental factors are acting and determining his attitude, decision-making processes and lifestyle of living in it.

The nature gives the people the resources we need to survive, for instance, fertile earth and a supply of water. The recourses are part of the environment. These resources determine the possibilities for mankind. Nature had it all under control. Humans had no control over the environment and could only use the given resources. Nature constrains in this way our activities.

Because of constrains, landscapes like the Rocky Mountains and the Alps are more preserved than landscapes like The Netherlands. People in those areas have less recourse available so their actions are more constrained than here.

Despite the fact that we can live everywhere on the globe, nature still determines a lot of our actions. For instance, we are still dependent on nature for the weather. We cannot control the weather. The weather is one example of how nature still determines our course of actions and therefore the landscape. Environmental determinism still influences and shapes the landscape, even if it plays a less important role as it used to. We are, and will always be dependent on the natural environment.

The German philosopher Immanuel Kant was also a determinist, who stated that the people of New Holland (Indonesia, East Indies) have half closed eyes and cannot see to any distance without bending their heads back until they touch their backs. This is due to the innumerable flies which are always flying in their eyes. Kant further stressed that all the inhabitants of hot lands are exceptionally lazy and timid. Timidity engenders superstition and in lands ruled by kings leads to slavery. Kant strongly argued for a scientific base to the study of geographical or environmental phenomena which he considered to be just as essential as the exact sciences. In support of his hypothesis of influence of climate, he stated that animals and men who migrate to other countries are gradually affected by their new environment. For example, the brown squirrels which migrate to Siberia turn grey and the colour of white cows in winter turns gray.

Friedrich Ratzel (1869) is considered the founder of environmental determinism in geography, and a pioneer in anthropogeography, which had three main aims: to describe the regions of the ecumene-habitable earth- and the distribution of mankind over it; to study human migratory movements of all types and their dependency on the land; to analyze the effects of the natural environment on the human body and spirit, both on individuals and entire social groups. He replaced 'classical' geographical determinism with the elements of Social Darwinism and propounded a theory of the state as an organism (Labensraum) which owed its life to the earth which was ever striving to seize more and more territory. Ratzel argued that "similar locations lead to similar mode of life". In support of his argument, he cited the example of British Isles and Japan and asserted that both these countries have insular locations, which provide natural defence against the invaders. Consequently, the people of these countries are making rapid economic progress, with the status of world powers. He was convinced that the course of history, the mode of life of the people, and the stage of development are closely influenced by the physical features and location of a place in relation to mountains and plains. In his deterministic approach, he gave more preference to location in relation to topographic features. He opined that location of a place determines the attitude and lifestyle of its people.

At the beginning of the 20th century, environmentalism became particularly widespread in the United States, where its leading proponents were Semple and Huntington. Semple was the direct descendent of Ratzel. She preached the philosophy of her master and thus was a staunch supporter of determinism. The book *Influence of Geographic Environment*, which she wrote, starts with the paragraph saying: "Man is a product of the earth's surface. This not only means that he is a child of the earth, dust of her dust; but that the earth has mothered him, fed him, set him tasks, directed his thoughts, contradicted him with difficulties that have strengthened his body and sharpened his wits, given him problems of navigation, of irrigation, and at the same time provided hints for their solution. She (The Earth) has entered into his bones and tissue, into his mind and soul. On the mountains she has given him leg muscles of iron to climb the slope; along the coast she has left these weak and flabby, but given him instead vigorous development of broad chest and powerful arms to handle his paddle or oar. In the river valleys, she attaches him to the fertile cultivating soil, circumscribes his ideas and ambitions by a dull round of calm, exacting duties and narrows his outlook to the cramped horizon of his land-farm. Upon the wide spread plateaus, in the boundless stretch of the grass-land and the waterless tracts of the desert, where he roams with his flocks from pasture and oasis to oasis, where life is much hardship but he escapes the grinds of drudgery, where the watching of grazing herd gives him leisure for contemplation, and the wide-ranging life of a big horizon. His ideas take on a certain gigantic simplicity, religion becomes monotheism and God becomes one, unrivaled, like the sand of the desert and the grass of the steppe, stretching out without break or change. Chewing over and the end of his simple belief as the one food of his unfed mind, his faith becomes fanaticism; his big ideas, born of that ceaseless regular legitimate fruit in wide imperial conquest."

However, Semple writes in her book and distinguishes the attitudinal characteristics of the people living in different physical settings, terrain, topographies and stresses that the people living in the mountains are essentially conservative. There is little in his environment to stimulate him to change and little reaches him from the outside world. Hence the innovative attribute is repugnant to him. Contrary to this, the people of plain parts of Europe are energetic, serious, thoughtful, rather than emotional, and cautious rather than impulsive. In the Mediterranean region where the climate is temperate and mild, the people are grey and imaginative and their life is easy going.

Huntington, the American philosopher's basic philosophy was that the supreme achievements of civilisation in any region were always bound up with a particular type of climate and variation in climate led to 'pulsations' in the history of culture. He suggested that the best climates for work were those in which there was variety and in which the temperatures fell within a certain range. The advancement of Europeans in the fields of science and technology has thus been attributed to climatic conditions by Huntington.

Teleological Approach

Teleological approach is in literal terms, the study of purposes, goals, or ends. In other words, this theory which acts, objects, states of affairs, and so on, can be justified only in terms of the ends towards which they are directed, or by the functions they fulfill. 'Rightness' is not intrinsic in an action or process, but it is dependent on the consequences of the action or the processes. For a simple example, the significance of a lioness stalking an antelope only becomes apparent when it is seen as directed to some other purpose, that is, of killing the antelope. In geography, Rostow's theory is teleological.

Regional geography finds its origins in the 19th century, which was greatly influenced by Darwin's work (Origin of Species, published in 1859), which broke the links between geography and natural theology and caused the rejection of geographical work, based on teleological approaches, laying the groundwork for new ways of conceptualising the relationship between human being and his environment, and heightening the interest in the region as a subject for geographical enquiry. However, Darwin's impact provided fresh stimulation for the doctrine of environmental determinism which controlled the human activities. This would explain the pattern and processes of human habitation of the earth's surface, and emphasises, which must be analyzed, are the effects of the natural environment on the human body and spirit of both individuals and entire living social groups.

Afterwards, regional geography developed from 19th-century originates from different directions. In the United States, regional geography is seen as a descriptive rather than a systematic study, while in Europe, regional geography can combine both aspects. In France, in particular, regional geography came to be associated with the work of Vidal de La Blache, who approached the concept of region from its human and cultural dimensions, seeing the region as the unique expression of the interaction between humanity and the physical environment. Regional approaches, initially very much influenced by environmental determinism, slowly moved within geographical studies in other directions, allowing for the study of the interaction between people and the environment without seeing causal links between the two, and offering human geographers a clear and well-defined object of study, having key themes as the concept of region and the interaction between people and the environment; in this way radically changing the discipline.

Possibilistic Approach

Vidal de La Blache was one of the speaking persons of environmental possibilities, which led to possibilism. Febvre was the main profounder of the concept of possibilism. This concept emphasises that physical environment is passive and man is the active Agent at liberty to choose between a wide range of environmental possibilities. According to possibilism, the pattern of human activity is the result of the initiative and mobility of man operating within the natural framework. Nowadays the role of natural elements in conditioning, though not controlling human activities, is often lost sight of. To counteract this degrading tendency and to rebuild the old Determinism on a newer footing, some leading geographers are preaching the determinists doctrines in an altered form, which approximates very closely to possibilism. It is the Stop and Go-Determinism propagated by Griffith Taylor, which means one should regulate one's activity as Red light acts for traffic regulations.

This approach was developed as a reaction to extreme generalisations of environmental determinists that led to a counter thesis, of possibilism which presented man as an active rather a passive agent. This is a philosophy which attempts to explain man and environment relationship in a different way, taking man as an active agent in the environment. This is a belief which asserts that natural environment provides options, the number of which increases as the knowledge and technology of a cultural group develop. This point of view was named 'possibilism' by Febvre, who wrote: "The true and only geographical problem is that of utilisation of possibilities. *There are no necessities, but everywhere possibilities*. The possibilists saw the physical environment a series of possibilities for human development, but argued that the actual ways in which development took place were related to the culture of the people concerned, except perhaps in regions of extremes like deserts, tundra, equatorial and high mountains.

The possibilists show with great precision that society interposes practices, beliefs, and rule of life between nature and man; that man's utilisation of possibilities and his exploitation of his environment are thereby hampered, so as, for example, to render his food singularly monotonous. Nowhere is food eaten by savages without care in the choice. There are prohibitions, restrictions, taboos on sides. But this social constraint was, no doubt, not exercised at first in its full vigour. There was great homogeneity in primitive human groups, but there were necessary differences (age and sex) and individual contingencies, however slight. In small societies the organisations were not rigid enough at the beginning to stifle initiative. It is thanks to differentiation, to the individual alone, that life has been ameliorated and that society itself has been organised.

The possibilists argued that it is impossible to explain the difference in human society and the history of that society with reference to the influence of physical environment. They hold that man himself brings his influence to bear on that environment and changes it.

Possibilistic Approach (19th and 20th Centuries)

The philosophy of possibilism believes that people are not just the products of their environment or just pawns of natural environment which became very much popular after the First World War. For the possibilists, the works of man, not the earth and its influence, are the starting points, the most important is the freedom of man to choose. Philosophy of possibilism became very much popular after the First World War. It was Vidal de Lablache who advocated and preached the philosophy of possibilism. Lablache was such a staunch supporter of this philosophy that he developed the 'school of possibilism'. Vidal in his studies minimised the influence of environment on the activities of man. In his opinions the human's lifestyles are the products and reflections of a civilisation, representing the integrated result of physical, historical, cultural and social influence surrounding man's relations to milieu in a particular place. He tried to explain differences between groups in the same or similar environment, and pointed out that these differences are not due to the dictates of physical environment but are the outcome of variations in attitudes, values and habits. Variations in attitudes and habits create numerous possibilities for human communities. It is this concept which became the basic philosophy of the school of possibilism.

The possibilists emphasise that it is impossible to explain the difference in human society and the history of that society with reference to the influence of environment; and they hold that man himself brings his influence to bear on that environment and change it.

According to the possibilistic approach, nature is only an adviser. In spite of the fact that man has numerous possibilities in a given physical setting, he cannot go against the directions laid by the physical environment. The possibilitic approach has been criticized by many of the contemporary thinkers. Griffith Taylor, while criticizing possibilism, stressed that society as a whole should make the choices, and since only an advisory role is assigned to geographer, his function "is not that of interpreting nature's plan". Taylor was largely right when he wrote that the task of geography is to study the natural environment and its effect on man, not all problems connected with man or the 'cultural landscape'. Moreover, possibilism does not encourage the study of geographical environment and it promotes over anthropocentrism in geography.

Geographic determinism at least obliges the geographer to turn his attention to nature, and if the question is asked as to who is setting out to destroy geography, then blame should be placed above all at the possibilists' door.

Economic Deterministic Approach

Economic deterministic approach is where human culture and free will have little place. It is also a spatial science deeply implicated in the capitalistic system and all of its associated inequalities, without any ability towards reproducing that society.

Economic determinism is the theory which gives primacy to the economic structure over politics in the development of human history. It is usually associated with the theories of Karl Marx, although many Marxist thinkers have dismissed plain and unilateral economic determinism as a form of "vulgar Marxism", or "economism", nowhere included in Marx's works.

Economic determinism as understood by Marxism is the belief that only the economical laws determine the course of human history.

The law of economic determinism attributed to Marx's materialisms simple, self-preservation or the pursuit of food, clothing, and shelter is the supreme instinct in man. Therefore, the argument in favour of economic determinism says, it is natural to expect that the overwhelming amount of the decisions made by people will involve their pursuit of food, clothing, and shelter. Furthermore, it is predictable that these decisions will be made in such a way that they will favour acquisition of food, clothing, or shelter. A decision made by an individual against food, clothing, or shelter would clearly be against that person's interest and would clearly be uncommon if not rare. As far as food, clothing, and shelter commodities are concerned which are bought and sold and traded in the society, the pursuit of these commodities is an economic activity.

According to Karl Marx, each social mode of production produces the materialistic conditions of its reproduction, i.e., ideology, which gathers all the political, law and cultural spheres. Thus, ideology allows the mode of production to reproduce itself. Furthermore, Karl Marx and Fredrik Engels are said to have believed that a revolutionary force will change the mode of production, and the dominant class will immediately set out to create a new society to protect this new economic order. In the modernity of their era, Marx and Engels felt that the propertied class had essentially accomplished the establishment of a new societal and economic order, instinctively creating a society which protects their capitalist interests. They made this argument to the Bourgeoisie in the Communist Manifesto, "Your very ideas are the outgrowth of conditions of your bourgeois production and bourgeois property, just as your jurisprudence is but the will of your class, made into law for all, a will whose essential characters and directions are determined by the economic conditions of the existence of your class." From this, it is argued that Marx and Engels did not believe men could arbitrarily choose any one of several forms of society, but only that one which promotes the prevailing mode of production. The nature of man's materialistic make-up requires him to do this.

However, the young Marxian hence criticised man's alienation, a concept which was later replaced by the critique of commodity fetishism. 'Vulgar Marxism' has considered that the relation between the economic infrastructure and the ideological superstructure was a uni-causal, and thus believed in economic determinism. This has been criticized by various Marxist theorists, who dismissed it as a form of economism or economic reductionism. They claimed that the relationship is much more reciprocal and complex than unilateral determinism would have it.

Many Marxists claimed that Marx and Engels viewed this law of 'economic determinism' as the creative force in human progress. Engels stated: "The final causes of all social changes and political revolution are to be sought, not in men's brains, not in man's insight into internal truth and justice... but in the economies of each epoch." Therefore, Engels advocated a change in economic structure as the only valid way of improving society and refining the intellectual make-up of humanity.

Ecological Approach

Ecology is the study of the interrelationships of living organisms and, especially, of groups of living organisms among themselves and between them and the non-living (or physical) environment. The ecological approach emphasizes on the relation between the organism and its environment and the relation between perception and action. It is a general theory of the perception and control of behaviour and general in the sense that it aspires to describe, explain, and predict perception and action by all animals in all situations, at all ages.

Ecological psychology has its root in the writings of James and Eleanor Gibson, who emphasised direct perception via the detection of higher-order stimulus variables, as opposed to a reductionist, constructivist-representational account of perception. The ecological approach focuses on the perception and control of animal's behaviours that occur naturally i.e., outside the laboratory. In particular, the ecological approach focuses on aspects of the animal and the environment that determine the success or failure of behaviours. The unit of analysis is the animal-environment system. Thus, it can be said that the ecological approach is a systems-based approach to the perception and control of action.

The Ecological Approach to Perception- a theoretical perspective on how animals, including humans, can be aware of their surroundings. It emphasises the relevance of activity to define the environment to be perceived.

Perception refers to observation of how animals, including humans, can be aware of their surroundings. The ecological approach to perception refers to a particular idea of how perception works and how it should be studied. The label "ecological" reflects two main themes that distinguish this approach from the establishment view. First, perception is an achievement of animal-environment systems, not simply animals (or their brains). What makes up the environment of a particular animal-cliffs or caves or crowds-is part of this theory of perception. Second, perception's main purpose is the guiding activity. So that a theory of perception cannot ignore what animals do. The kinds of activities that a particular animal does-how it eats and moves and mates-are part of this theory of perception. Including the environment and behaviour as important factors of perceptual theory, rather than as after thoughts, it is clearly different from theories that start inside the eye or the ear or the skin, but it is not necessarily controversial.

Nonetheless, the ecological approach is considered controversial because of one central claim that the perception is direct. In order to understand this claim, and why some might consider it troublesome, we need to contrast it with the more traditional view. Most scholars and scientists believe that perception begins with faulty input. For example, when objects in the world reflect light, the pattern of light that reaches the back of the eye which is called the retina, has lost and distorted a lot of detail. Then the job of perception becomes one of fixing the input and adding more meaningful interpretations to it so that the brain can come to a conclusion about what caused that input in the first place. This is called indirect perception because the animal's awareness of the world is a result of these intermediary steps. The theory of direct perception, in contrast, argues that the intermediary steps are only needed if the scientist has described the input incorrectly. Including the environment and activity into the theory of perception, it allows a better description of the input, a description that shows the input to be richly structured by the environment and the animal's own activities. This means that the intermediary steps are not required and perception is direct. There is a reciprocal relationship between environment and living organisms. In other words, environment provides habitats of varying kinds for different life forms and affects the lifestyle of various organisms in different habitats having distinct assemblages of land, water, soil and climate, and in turn organisms affect and modify the environment.

This sort of mutual relationship makes the natural ecosystem more efficient. Of all the organisms, man is the most intelligent and powerful animal and is capable of not only affecting the environment like other organisms but affecting the basic composition of the environment at a scale detrimental not only to all biota but also to his own existence. Phenomenal increase in human population in the present century has put enormous pressure on natural resources which has resulted into accelerated rate of rapacious exploitation of natural resources in order to meet demands of the ever-increasing population, rapidly growing industrialisation and urbanisation.

The developments of modern technologies and increased economic functions have further accelerated the rate of exploitation of natural resources. All these have contributed to the depletion or near depletion of a few precious non-renewable resources, degeneration of renewable resources (e.g., forest, grasslands, surface and groundwater etc.), environmental degradation and pollution at local, regional and global levels and above all ecological crisis. Environmentalists stress upon a symbiosis between man and the environment so that harmonious relationship may be established which may lead to the welfare of the human society.

It is, therefore, very important for environmental science to study the direct and indirect impacts of human activities on environmental/ physical and biological processes, which lead to ecosystem's instability and environmental degradation and pollution, the capacity and mechanism of natural/physical processes to absorb and adjust with the changes brought by man in the natural environment and to make sincere efforts for the identification and determination of levels of environmental degradation, pollution and ecological imbalance at different spatial and temporal scales, for the identification of real ecological and environmental crises, for the preparation of inventory of existing ecological resources, for the formulation of pollution control programme and conservation and management of natural resources, considering the fact into that all the resources, renewable and even nonconventional (even the solar energy are also finite because the life of the sun is also fixed), are finite and we have moral obligations to our future generations.

Chapter - 2

Environment and Society

The phenomenon of environment is described as the natural world of land, water, air, plants and animals that exist around us. It forms the basis of our existence and development. Environmental studies deal with every aspect which affects living organism. It is essentially a multidisciplinary approach that brings about an appreciation of our natural world and human impact on environmental integrity. Almost about ten thousand years ago, when mankind changed from a hunter-gatherer living, living in wilderness area such as forests and grasslands, into agriculturalists and pastoralists, we started making change to the environment which suit our own requirements. As our ability to grow food and use domestic animals developed, these 'natural' ecosystems were ultimately converted into agricultural land. However, the most traditional agriculturists depend extensively on natural resources like, rain, streams and rivers for water. Later on, they began to use wells to tap underground water sources and to impound water and created agricultural land for irrigation by building dams. Recently, we have begun to use chemical fertilisers and pesticides to further boost the yield from the same amount of land. However, we are now realising that all this has led to several undesirable changes in our environment. Mankind has been overexploiting and depleting natural resources. The over-intensive use of land has exhausted the capability of the ecosystem to support the growing demands of more and more people, all requiring more intensive use of resources. Industrial growth, urbanisation, population growth and enormous increase in the use of consumer goods, have further stressed the environment, as they create great quantities of solid waste. Air, water and soil pollution, in turn, have begun to severely affect human health. The result of transformation of natural resources from the wilderness ecosystems and agricultural sector to the urban user has led to a serious inequality in the distribution of these natural resources among human beings, which is both unfair and unsustainable.

Natural Environment

In the past decade or so, more and more attention is being paid all over the world to man's impact upon environment on which human depends and the maintenance of which is now increasingly being considered as essential for the welfare of mankind.

Thus, by environment we meant those natural things that surround us, the essentials to sustain human life, such as the earth's atmosphere, healthy air and drinkable water, together with the non-essentials that help to make life sustainable, such as wild animals or wild places or human living space.

With the passage of time, mankind is realising that preserving the essential ingredients of life and the rich natural diversity of the planet is indeed worthwhile. Thus, protecting and saving the environment involves keeping Nature's gifts to mankind as much as possible, and in as good a condition as practicable.

Pollution, especially in the industrialised belt, and urban areas and the ecological crisis are not wholly new or novel, though ecology is a comparatively new arena of science. The idea behind the preservation of natural resources is, however, almost as old as man.

Now the realisation about the loss of humanity that we have been destroying valuable resources, there must be a limit to our plans and ambitions for the development and growth. Murder of the environment involves senseless poisoning of our earth, air and water, and destruction of forest resource, may be described as "ecocide".

Most of our rivers like, the Ganga and the Yamuna, are polluted. The Himalayan ecology is seriously endangered in many ways. The consequences of such continuous and careless use of trees and other environmental natural resources would be disastrous. There are also the dangers from chemical pollution, from radio-active wastes, and other wastes from industrial houses, hospitals and chemical laboratories, and from other foreign matter that keeps on entering into the atmosphere. It is a speculation by the experts that if the energy of the sun is hindered, if the natural processes of purification and elimination are reversed, and if the reckless destruction and pollution continue, mankind may return to the dreaded ice age.

Therefore, preservation and restoration of the natural balance is vital and efforts are being made for the same purpose, at local, national and international levels.

For the first time a systematic and international effort in this direction was taken in 1972 through the UN Conference on Environment, which was held in Stockholm. The world's ecological mess was discussed there for several days. But by that year merely 10 nations had formulated environment protection programmes and now the number is above 100.

A significant development has been made by the by the Third World that the advanced countries like, USA and certain other western countries are misinterpreting the pollution problem and ignoring its dangers as an excuse for going slow in industrialising the backward and developing regions.

Some of the unpleasant facts that are deepening the ecological crisis are that about 12,000 new hazardous chemicals are being introduced into the world annually; some deserts have been spreading vastly and encroaching at the rate of 30 kilometers annually; some oceans are reported to be dying and the earth's protective ozone layer is being depleted by CFCs, aerosols and supersonic aero-planes.

Air, water and land are, after all, limited resources and cannot be largely used up for long time. The economists, therefore, warn that these must be viewed as capital, that must be preserved and protected and should not be considered as sources of additional income.

Following the dawning of the realities and better knowledge of the disaster looming ahead, there is greater awareness of the need for environmental education and for which millions of educated people have begun to regard as a matter of life and death. The developed and advanced industrial countries may even be said to be "exporting" their pollution problems to the Third World by decentralising and selling out their production processes and establishing factories in other parts of the world.

Such industrial factories are being welcomed by the under-developed and developing countries because of the employment opportunities they provide. However, further evidence of the growing international recognition of the importance of ecology has been provided by the adoption by the United Nations, in October, 1982, of a world Charter for nature which is aimed at preserving and protecting all species existing on earth. The Charter says that mankind is totally dependent on natural systems for food, energy and nutrients, and civilisation is rooted in nature. "Every form of life is unique, warrants respect, regardless of its worth to human beings." The Charter further adds that "population levels of all forms of life, wild and domesticated, must be at least sufficient space for their survival, and to this end necessary habitats must be maintained. Nature shall be preserved and secured against the environmental degradation caused by warfare or other hostile activities, military activity damaging to nature should be avoided." The Charter adds that all "governments shall co-operate in the task of conserving nature and make sure that activities within their jurisdiction or control do not cause damage to natural systems located within their States."

However, the government of India has constituted a new Department of Environment on November 1, 1980, under the charge of the Prime Minister, to make an in-depth review of the administrative machinery for the legislative measures for environmental protection.

The Department of Environment serves as the coordinating agency for activities related to environmental protection and management. The Botanical Survey of India and the Zoological Survey of India have been kept under the administrative control of the new Department for which a National Committee on Environmental Planning (NCEP) has also been constituted.

Until recently, the dangers and extent of environmental pollution in India were not realised, although there are certain scientists, who had warned India, that unless timely steps were taken, this country too would have to face the problems confronting the Western regions.

The rapid growth of industrialisation, the discharge of untreated polluted waste, the effluents, the widespread neglect of environment, the resulted outcome of pollution through human ignorance and use

City Life: Society environment Interaction

of open spaces near rivers as public conveniences is resulting in the severe pollution of major rivers, estuaries, sea-fronts, creeks and water channels.

Thus, there is increasing atmospheric pollution which is especially noticeable in cities like Mumbai, Kolkata, Kanpur, Ahmadabad and other industrial complexes, notably those, where chemical industries have been set up and proper safety measures have not been enforced.

However, India has reached at a stage when the absorptive and assimilative capacities have been overused or misused, resulting in environmental pollution and environmental degradation. It is also true that the natural environment has an enormous potential capacity to accept and absorb most wastes; what is discarded by one species is often used up by another. But with emerging more industrial centers in many States, and releasing of chimneys dark smoke and coal-dust into the atmosphere, and the drains getting choked with hazardous chemical and poisonous wastes, the dangers of pollution are increasing day by day.

The problem of improving the quality of the environment is basically economic. It follows the failure of the market system to allocated environmental resources efficiently. It has also to be noted that the ultimate measure of environmental quality is the value the people place on it and the extent to which they are willing to pay to maintain it.

The protective remedies are: providing alternative to the production processes, by installing anti-pollution equipments and reusing or recycling wastes. However, some years ago, the Associated Chambers of Commerce and Industry carried out a study of industrial pollution.

The findings and recommendations were thought to be very useful, i.e., (a) the industrial pollution must be regularly monitored and it must become an integral part of business planning, (b) there is also, lack of awareness about the concern the dangers of pollution in the Indian-corporate sectors. Pollution control is, however, in essence, a managerial and corporate responsibility and requires good house-keeping and appropriate preventive measures; (c) there must be a legal and institutional arrangement to permit efficient and politically responsible implementation.

The problems with the Indian administrative set up have been found in the area of Five-Year Plans, which is that the ambitious plans are drawn up, ample funds are allocated and there is much fanfare, but there are no proper criteria of implementing the programmes. On the other hand, implementations of anti-pollution programs in Britain, France, Germany and the USA have been proved to be very effective and there is a growing awareness of the hazards of pollution.

In India, it is necessary to have a national commitment for preventing our environment from environmental pollution. For this purpose, there should be proper co-operation among the Centre, the various State Governments, and local governments and business and the people in general.

However, there are various ways of publicity which needs to be carried out to inculcate the proper habits among the people and the proper industrial practices. Incentives in this regard would be a good national investment. Strict laws should be enforced to control the tree felling and destruction of foliage. Tolerance of unclean air, water and smoke must be discouraged at each level.

For example, the USA is spending billions of dollars on pollution control. The environment in that country has significantly improved. India need not has to spend as much because the extent of the menace of environmental pollution is still within control (the country being largely agricultural), but timely measures can save much distress and hazards to health caused by the rapid pace of modernisation and industrialisation in urban areas.

Society–Environment Interaction

As we know that, a living organism cannot live by itself in isolation. Organisms interact among themselves. Hence, all organisms, such as plants, animals and human beings, as well as the physical environmental surroundings with whom we interact, form a part of our natural environment. All these constituents of the environment are dependent upon each other. Thus, they maintain a balance in nature. And we are the only organisms who try to modify the environment to fulfill our needs. Thus, it is our responsibility to take necessary steps to control the environmental imbalances.

All human beings are endowed by nature to be reflective and active. Their biological evolution gives them potential capacity to create tools and establish an adaptive relationship with nature. In the beginning, human life was more biological than social and cultural and was somewhat similar to other animals where environmental considerations dictated the place of human residence. However, in the process of adaptive relationship, man gradually evolved tools with the help of which the natural resources of the natural environment could be put to use. The ability to make tool of human beings developed over a very long period of time as it began with the use of materials locally obtainable. The tools shaped human life in such a way that we witness the emergence and growth of cultures.

The different stages of human culture have been identified on the basis of the tools used by them. The earliest was the paleolithic age representing the beginning of the tool industry. In this age humans lived by gathering plant foods and hunting animals. It was inherent in the nature of the economy of the period that humans could not lead sedentary life and were forced to migrate to new places in search of plant foods and game. This kind of life-style restricted the size of the peregrinating human groups. It can be firmly argued that during this stage of human history the environment dictated terms and humans had just started to modify their dependence on nature. Nonetheless, it is necessary to point out that human's mobility had led to greater interaction between numerous groups of humans spread over different parts of the world.

Man creates influences on the society. Conditions which are favourable for supporting life help in increase in the number of lives. Man tries to enhance his change through the change of environment. Man tries to change the environment through agricultural, industry and industrialisation, urbanisation etc. mobilisation of natural resources for betterment of human life has helped in the human population growth. The use of fertilisers, pesticides etc. is gaining popularity for increasing the production of crops. The residue of the same causes environmental pollution. But the development of the scientific method of food production, transportation and storage facilities have made the food available throughout the year at any place on the earth and these are most important for the existence of human beings. Industrialisation also helps in movement of people to large cities from rural areas for their livelihood. This is one of the causes for development of new cities where people begin to concentrate in large number.

The population increases at a rapid rate due to increasing fertility rate and decreasing mortality. On the other hand, industrialisation gives rise to production of more waste materials which are responsible for the pollution of air, water and soil. Polluted environment has its effect on the health of human beings. This is how natural resources at one end help in the growth of human population but at the other end environmental pollution due to excessive utilisation of natural resources creates problem in the environment.

Pollution–Environment Interaction

The greatest problem that the world is facing today is that of severe environmental pollution, which is increasing with every passing year and causing grave and irreparable damage to the earth.

Environmental pollution is thus can be said that any discharge of material or energy into water, land, or air that causes or may cause acute or chronic detriment to the Earth's ecological balance or that declines the quality of life. Environmental pollutants may cause primary damage, with direct identifiable impact on the environment, or secondary damage in the form of minor perturbations in the delicate balance of the biological food chain that are detectable only over long time periods.

Pollution is the effect of undesirable changes in our surroundings that have harmful effects on plants, animals and human beings. This however, occurs, when the interests of short-term economic gains are made at the cost of long-term ecological benefits for humanity. No phenomenon has led to greater ecological changes than has been

Water Pollution

made by mankind. During the last few decades we have contaminated our air, water and land on which life itself totally depends with a variety of waste products.

Till now, in the history of humanity, where pollution has existed, it has been primarily a local problem. The growing industrialisation in society, the introduction of motorised vehicles, and the explosion of the human population, however, have caused an exponential growth in the production of goods and services. Coupled with this growth has been a tremendous increase in waste by-products. The indiscriminate discharge of untreated industrial and domestic wastes into waterways, the spewing of thousands of tonnes of particulates and airborne gases into the atmosphere, the "throwaway" attitude toward solid wastes, and the use of newly developed chemicals without considering potential consequences have resulted in major environmental disasters, including the formation of smog in the Los Angeles area since the late 1940s and the pollution in large areas of the Mediterranean Sea. Advancement in technology has begun to solve some pollution problems, and public awareness of the extent of pollution will eventually force governments to undertake more effective environmental planning and adopt more effective antipollution measures.

Environmental pollution thus can be defined as any undesirable change in physical, chemical and biological characteristics of our air, land and water. As a result of over-population, population explosion, rapid industrialisation, and other human activities like agriculture and deforestation etc., earth was loaded with diverse pollutants that were released as by-products. Pollutants are generally grouped under two classes:

(a) **Biodegradable pollutants -** Biodegradable pollutants are degraded by the activity of micro-organisms and enter into the cycles of biogeochemical. Examples of such pollutants are domestic waste products, urine and faucal matter, sewage, agricultural residue, paper, wood and cloth etc.

(b) **Non-Biodegradable pollutants -** Non-biodegradable pollutants do not break down easily into simpler and harmless products. They have stronger chemical bandage. These include various insecticides and other pesticides, mercury, lead, arsenic, aluminum, plastics, radioactive waste etc.

Different Types of Pollution

Pollution can be broadly classified according to the components of environment that are polluted. Major of these are: Air pollution, Water pollution, Soil pollution (land degradation), Thermal pollution, Noise pollution, Pesticide pollution and Radiation pollution etc. Details of these types of pollutions are discussed in unit-3 with their preventive measures.

- Air pollution is the concentration of harmful gases in the atmosphere that, affect human health or produce other measured effects on living matter and other materials.
- Water pollution is any undesirable change in water quality that adversely affects living organisms or makes water unsuitable for their use.
- Land pollution is the degradation of the Earth's surface through faulty use of the soil by faulty agricultural practices, mineral exploitation, industrial waste dumping, and indiscriminate disposal of urban wastes.

- Noise pollution is a make-up and composite of sounds generated by human activities ranging from blasting, horn or stereo systems to the roar of ballistic missile or supersonic transport jets.

Human demands are ever increasing with the growth of population and advancement of modernity, but the natural resources at disposal are limited. Reckless and careless exploitation of natural resources is causing a serious imbalance. The natural environment has started giving way. However, the spread of vast desertification, soil erosion, floods, droughts, urban congestion and extinction or threat of extinction of countless species of fauna and flora are the visible phenomena "affecting" the ecosystem and causing pollution of land, water and air.

The demands for food, shelter, clothing, energy and other basic human needs have been increasing to the crisis point. In case these natural resources, if not managed and used properly, will become impossible to provide for the quality of life of human beings.

Therefore, the environment which provides the resources for supporting the population and achieves development has to be managed through protection and conservation.

Technology–Environment Interaction

Environment provides its people all the possible means to utilise the existing resources for their betterment. Technology in this way gains the dominant role to fulfill human needs. Throughout the history, human with the help of different types of technologies has used the environment for his sustenance and adapted the same for the development of the society. With the increasing technological advancement man has altered his demand which is not conventional but non-conventional. With the limited source of conventional energy (i.e. coal, petroleum, gas etc) to fulfill the growing needs of increasing population, man has used different types of technologies to utilise non-conventional energy (i.e., solar energy, wind energy, hydro energy, biomass energy, biogas energy, geothermal energy etc.). The unscientific use of conventional energy resources like, coal, petroleum etc. has led to numerous environmental problems. Hence there is emphasis on sustainable development. Sustainable development is the process of development of the available resources with the present available technologies for development without compromising the future needs of the society.

Energy can be defined by the physicists as the capacity of an individual to do work. Energy is found on our planet in various forms, some of which are immediately useful, while others require a process of transformation.

Environmental technology or sustainable use of technology is the application of one or more of environmental science such as green chemistry, environmental monitoring and electronic devices to monitor, model and conserve the available natural environment and environmental resources, and to check the negative impacts of human involvement. This term is also used to describe sustainable energy generation technologies like, solar energy, wind energy, biogas energy, biomass energy, hydro-energy, bioreactors, etc. Sustainable development is the core of *environmental technology*. The term *environmental technology* is also used to describe a class of electronic devices that can promote sustainable management of resources.

India has a land of vast supply of green or renewable energy resources, and it has one of the largest programmes in the world for deploying renewable energy products and systems. Indeed, it is the only country in the world to have a separate ministry for renewable energy development called the Ministry of Non-Conventional Energy Sources (MNES). Since its inception, the Ministry has launched one of the world's largest and most ambitious programmes on renewable energy. Based on various promotional efforts put in place by MNES, significant progress is being made in power generation from renewable energy sources. MNES has been renamed the Ministry of New and Renewable Energy.

Solar energy

Solar energy is an important source of alternative form of energy, although currently it is underutilised. Also, a form of energy resource in India with the potential to offer an improved power supply especially in remote areas and increase the security of India's demand for increasing energy supply. On an average, India has 300 sunny days per annum and receives an average hourly radiation of 200 MW/km^2. The India Energy Portal estimates that around 12.5% of India's land mass, or 413,000 km^2, could be used for utilisation and harnessing solar energy.

Solar energy is an abundant and renewal energy resource. The annual solar energy incident at the ground in India is about 20,000 times the current electrical energy consumption. The utilisation of solar energy in India has been very limited. This is because solar energy is a dilute energy source with average daily solar energy incident in India 5 kWh/m^2 per day, and hence energy must be collected over vast areas resulting in high initial capital investment. It is also an intermittent source of energy. Hence solar energy must incorporate storage in order to take care of energy needs during nights and on cloudy days. This results in further increase in the capital of investment cost of such systems. One way to overcome this problem is to use a large body of water for the collection and storage of solar energy. This concept is called as solar pond.

National Institute of Solar Energy has assessed the Country's solar potential of about 748 GW assuming 3% of the waste land area to be covered by Solar PV modules. Solar energy has taken a central place in India's National Action Plan on Climate Change with National Solar Mission as one of the key Missions. National Solar Mission (NSM) was launched on 11th January, 2010. NSM is a major initiative of the Government of India with active participation from States to promote ecological sustainable growth while addressing India's energy security challenges. It will also constitute a major contribution by India to the global effort to meet the challenges of climate change. The Mission's objective is to establish India as a global leader in solar energy by creating the policy conditions for solar technology diffusion across the country as quickly as possible. The Mission targets installing 100 GW grid-connected solar power plants by the year 2022. This is line with India's Intended Nationally Determined Contributions (INDCs) target to achieve about 40 percent cumulative electric power installed capacity from non-fossil fuel-based energy resources and to reduce the emission intensity of its GDP by 33 to 35 percent from 2005 level by 2030.

State-wise estimated Solar Energy Potential in the Country (Annual Report 2019-20)

Sr. No.	States/UTs	Solar Potential (GWp) #
1.	Andhra Pradesh	38.44
2.	Arunachal Pradesh	8.65
3.	Assam	13.76
4.	Bihar	11.20
5.	Chhattisgarh	18.27
6.	Delhi	2.05
7.	Goa	0.88
8.	Gujarat	35.77
9.	Haryana	4.56
10.	Himachal Pradesh	33.84
11.	Jammu Kashmir	111.05
12.	Jharkhand	18.18
13.	Karnataka	20.70
14.	Kerala	6.11
15.	Madhya Pradesh	61.66
16.	Maharashtra	64.32
17.	Manipur	10.63
18.	Meghalaya	5.86
19.	Mizoram	9.09
20.	Nagaland	7.29
21.	Odisha	25.78
22.	Punjab	2.81
23.	Rajasthan	142.31
24.	Sikkim	4.941
25.	Tamil Nadu	7.61
26.	Telangana	20.41
27.	Tripura	2.08
28.	Uttar Pradesh	22.83
29.	Uttarakhand	16.80
30.	West Bengal	6.26
31.	UTs	0.79
	TOTAL	**748.98**

 # Assessed by National Institute of Solar Energy.

India is located between the Tropic of Cancer and the Equator, and hence has an average annual temperature that ranges from 25°C – 27.5 °C. This means that India has huge solar potential. The sunniest parts are situated in the south/east coast, from Kolkata to Chennai. Solar energy has multiple applications like, photovoltaic (PV) cells can be placed on the roof top of houses or commercial buildings and collectors such as mirrors or parabolic dishes that can move and track the sun throughout the day are also used. This mechanism is being used for concentrated lighting in buildings.

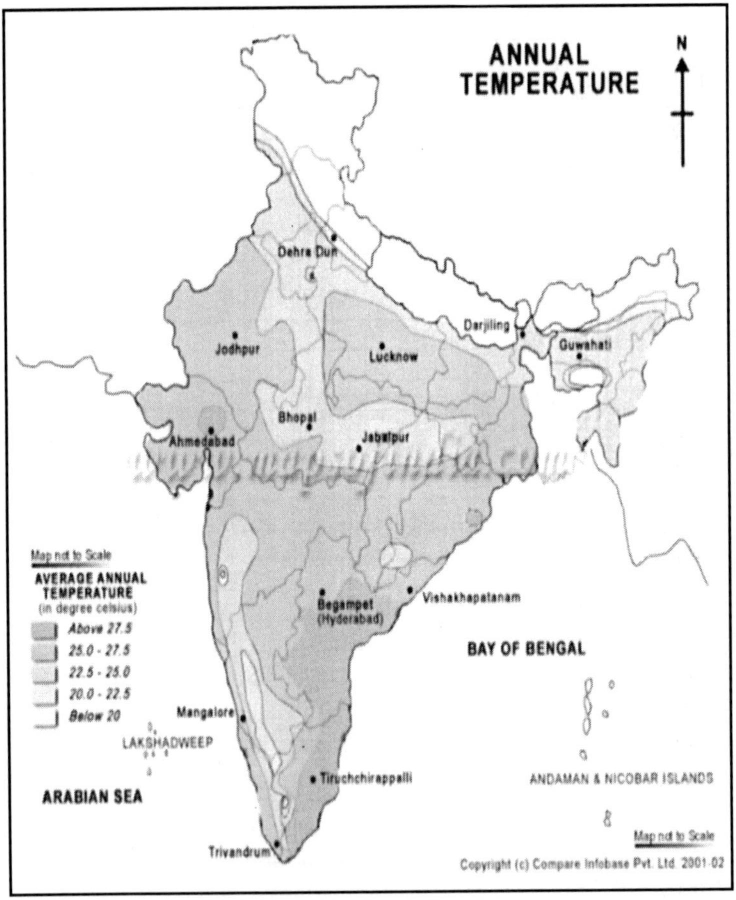

Source: http://www.mapsofindia.com/maps/india

Photovoltaic (PV) cells have a low efficiency factor, yet power generation systems using photovoltaic materials have the advantage of having no moving parts. Photovoltaic cells find applications in individual home rooftop systems, community street lights, community water pumping, and areas where the terrain makes it difficult to access the power grid. The efficiency of solar photovoltaic cells with single crystal silicon is about 13%-17%. High efficient cells with concentrators are being manufactured which can operate with low sunlight intensities.

Wind energy: Estimated Wind Power Potential in India

State	Gross Potential (MW)
Andhra Pradesh	9063
Gujarat	7362
Karnataka	7161
Kerala	1026
Madhya Pradesh	4978
Maharashtra	4519
Odisha	1520
Rajasthan	6672
Tamil Nadu	4159
West Bengal	32
TOTAL	46,092
Total No. of Stations in operation at the end of February 2006	59
Total No. of Stations closed down in March 2006	1
Total No. of Stations Commissioned in March 2006	1
Total No. of Stations in operation as on 31st March 2006	59

The potential power of wind on a national level, base data collected from 10 states considering only 1% of land availability, is around 46,092 MW.

Wind energy is another alternative form of energy. In the production of wind energy, India is surpassed only by Germany as one of the world's fastest growing markets for wind energy. By the mid-1990s, the subcontinent was installing more wind generating capacity than North America, Denmark, Britain, and the Netherlands.

The installations of ten machines near Okha in the province of Gujarat were some of the first wind turbines installed in India. These 15-meter Vestas wind turbines overlook the Arabian Sea. Now, in

2006, there was an installed capacity of 4,430 MW; however, ten times that potential, or 46,092 MW, exists.

For the installation of a wind farm, the capital cost ranges between 4.5 crores to 5.5 crores, depending on the site and the wind electric generator (WEG) selected for installation.

However, the Indian Government has outlined ambitious capacity of expansion and investment plans for the period (2007- 2012) and wind power projects form the majority of the proposed capacity addition. The total investments on development of renewal energy during the plan period is expected to be more than $15 billion (~Rs. 60,000 crores). The majority of this investment is being raised through domestic private investors, concessional financing from specialised government agencies and multilateral financial institutions.

With the increasing awareness of the use and benefits of wind power and evolving government priorities more banks and lending institutions are showing interest in funding these projects. On top of the financing spectrum is the Indian Renewable Energy Development Agency (IREDA), which is the apex nodal agency for renewable energy development in India and a funding arm of MNRE. The other government agencies that actively fund renewable energy projects are the Power Finance Corporation (PFC) and Rural Electrification Corporation (REC).

The multilateral agencies such as the World Bank, the International Finance Corporation (IFC), and the Asian Development Bank (ADB), as well as bi-lateral agencies such as KFW (German Development Bank) have also stepped up their assistance to the sector in the last few years. Prominent domestic banks that fund renewable projects are IDBI, ICICI, IFCI, SBI and PNB among others. Foreign banks such as Standard Chartered, RBS India (formerly known as ABN Amro) and Rabo bank are also providing renewable energy project financing.

However, India's current market for the Renewal energy business is growing at an annual rate of 15%. The scope for private investment in Renewal energy is estimated to grow at about $3 billion per annum. Given the evolving regulatory and policy regime, the business outlook is generally positive at this time. The Government's proposed policy guidance and regulations are also coming into place to further strengthen this rate of growth.

Chhadvel wind farm in Dhule, Maharashtra

Advantages of Wind Power:

- It is one of the most environment friendly, clean and safe energy resources.
- It has the lowest development period as compared to conventional energy.
- Equipment structure and commissioning need only a few months.
- There is no energy consumption, hence low operating costs.
- Maintenance costs are low.
- The capital cost is comparable with conventional power plants.

Wind Energy in India:

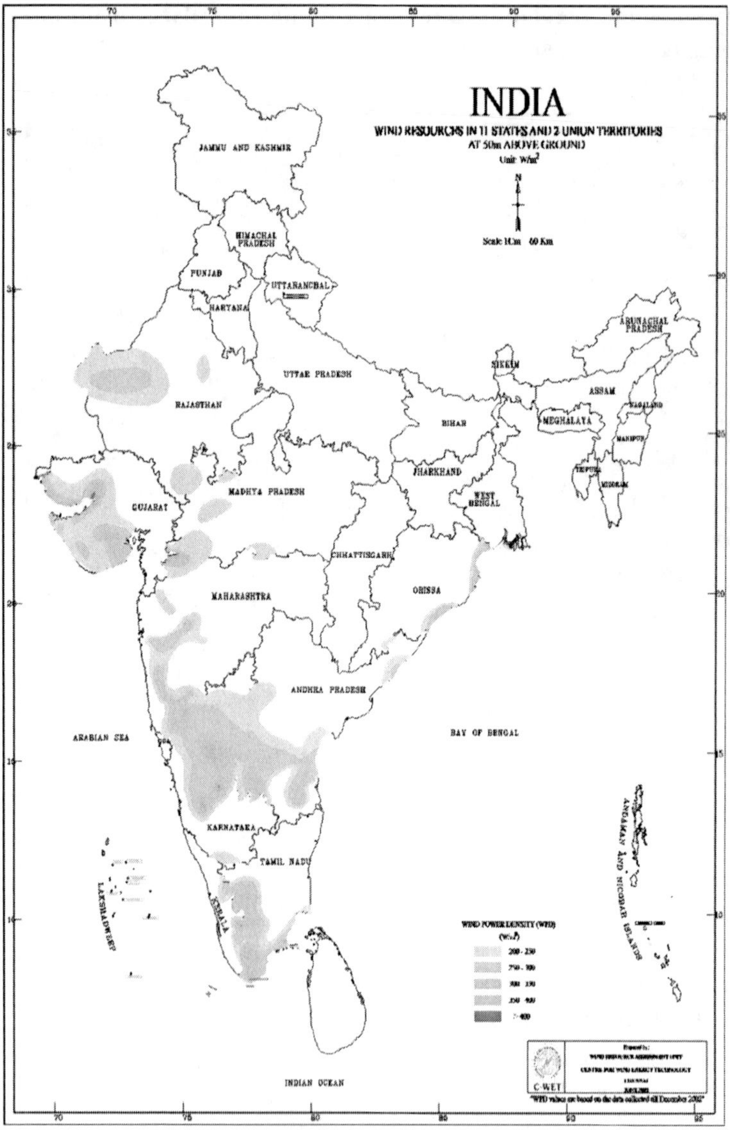

Source: http://www.cwet.tn.nic.in/html/departments_wpdmap.html#

An area where a number of wind electric generators are installed is known as a wind farm.

The essential requirements for establishment of a wind farm for optimal exploitation of the wind are the following:

- High wind resource at particular site.
- Adequate land availability.
- Suitable terrain and good soil condition.
- Maintenance access to site.
- Suitable power grid nearby.
- Techno-economic selection of specific turbines.
- Scientifically prepared.

The generation of wind energy has limitations which will influence the extent and type of role it will ultimately play in overall generation of electricity in India.

Hydro energy

Hydro energy has a vast potential of providing alternative energy in India. India is enforced for large deployment of hydropower in present conducive policy and investment environment. With the growing demand of energy and concern for carbon emission is making hydropower development more favourable. The Indian Government is ensuring a good performance of the new Small Hydro Power (SHP) stations by linking the incentives to the SHP developers with the performance of the station.

The estimated potential for small hydro power in India of 15,000 MW suggests that it can make a significant contribution to India's power supply, especially in remote areas where alternative supply solutions face many challenges. For these reasons, the further development of small hydro power is one of the focal areas of MNRE, who wants to concentrate on reducing the capital costs and enhancing the reliability, plant load factors, and average plant lifetimes. The Indian government aims to develop half of the identified potential in the next 10 years and is supporting small-hydro power station deployment through capital subsidies and preferential tariffs. As of

March 2010, a total of 2,735 MW of grid-connected small hydropower has been installed, contributing about 16.2% to India's total grid interactive renewable power.

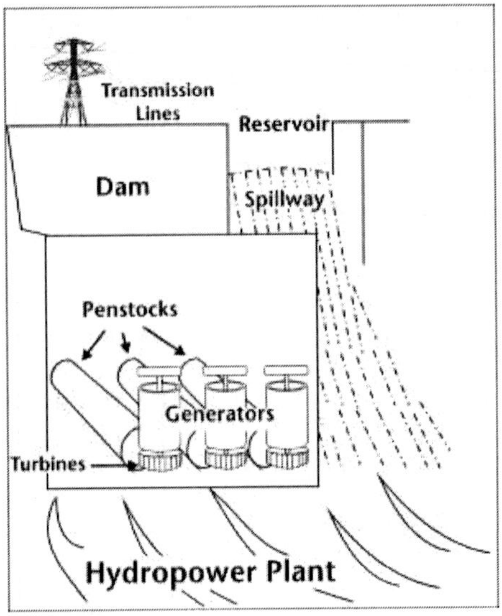

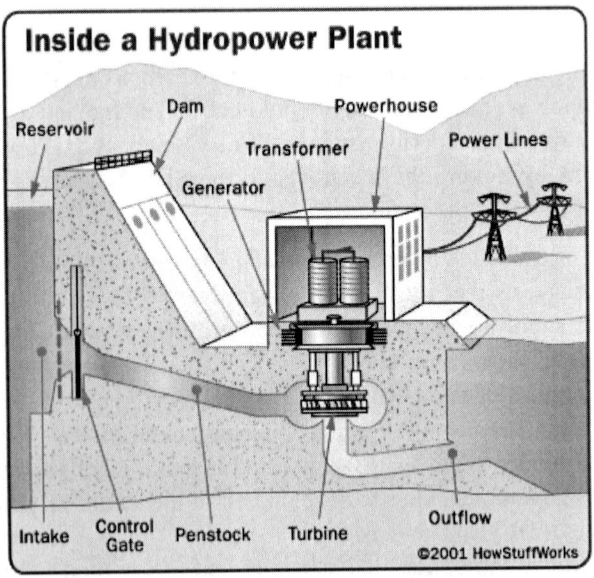

In India, small hydro plants have a capacity of 25 MW or less and are further subdivided into micro (100 kW or less), mini (between 100 kW and 2 MW), and small (between 2 MW and 25 MW). Large hydropower plant is not covered in this paper. Small hydropower plants are generally run-of-river, with only small amounts of water stored, if any. These projects are considered environmentally favourable, particularly when compared to large hydro plants with storage reservoirs, which can cause habitat destruction and community displacement.

MNRE's 2019–2020 Annual Report estimated potential of small/mini/micro hydel projects in the country is 21133.65 MW from 7133 sites located in different States of India. The SHP projects in the country are being set-up both in public and private sectors. Setting up of SHP projects normally require about 3-4 years depending upon its size and location. The national target for SHP is to achieve a cumulative capacity of 5000 MW by 2022, under overall targets of achieving a cumulative grid connected Renewable Energy Power Projects of 175,000 MW. Against this target of achieving an aggregate capacity of 5000 MW by the year 2022, an aggregate capacity of 4671.557 MW been achieved by 31st December 2019 through 1127 small hydropower projects.

Advantages of Hydropower Plant:

- It is totally renewable and non-polluting and can also provide a more stable price regime over a long period of time.
- It has an intrinsic capability for quick starting, stopping, load variations, etc. and is thus ideally suited for meeting out the peak demand.
- Production cost is not only inflation free but it also reduces with time.
- Development of hydropower projects is also associated with various purposes like, irrigation, drinking water, flood control, navigation and tourism benefits.
- Pumped storage plants can be effectively regulated. Hence the energy can be used when needed. It can also quickly reverse its mode of operation from pumping to generating

and vice versa. Thus, pumped storage plants can play significant role in meeting out the peak demand and also in improving the grid stability and load factor of thermal power stations.

- The environmental impact of small hydro plants would be ideally suited for rural electrification and particularly in remote areas.

Biogas energy

Biogas is an easily available form of energy resource. It is produced from plant material, animal waste, garbage, waste from households and some types of industrial wastes, such as fish processing, dairies, and sewage treatment plants. It is a mixture of various gases which includes methane, carbon dioxide, hydrogen sulphide and water vapour. The product of anaerobic digestion is a mixed gas primarily composed of methane and carbon dioxide which commonly is called biogas. Methane is burnt easily in this mixture. From 1 tonne of food waste, one can produce 85 Cu. M of biogas. Once used, the residue can be used as an agriculture fertiliser.

Country like, Denmark produces a large quantity of biogas from waste and produces 15,000 MW of electricity from 15 farmers' cooperatives. However, London has a plant which makes 30 MW of electricity a year from 420,000 tonnes of municipality waste, which supplies power to over 50,000 families. In Germany, 25% of the landfills for garbage produce power from biogas; Japan also uses 85% of its waste in a similar way to supply power and France about 50%.

Thus, biogas plants have become highly popular in India and particularly in the rural sector. The biogas plants use cow-dung that is converted into a gas which is used as a fuel. It is also used for running dual fuel engines. The reduction in kitchen smoke by using biogas has reduced lung problems in thousands of homes.

In small scale installations the gas is primarily utilised for heating and cooking. In larger units CHP's are fueled with biogas. In any case, the driving force for the gas utilisation was to economize fossil fuels or wood as in developing countries.

The fibrous waste of the sugar industry is the world's largest potential source of biomass energy. Ethanol produced from sugarcane molasses is a good automobile fuel and is now used in a third energy resource of the vehicles in Brazil.

The National Project on Biogas Development (NPBD) and Community/Institutional Biogas Plant Programme promote various biogas projects. In 1996, there were already 2.18 million families in India that used biogas. However, China has over 20 million households using biogas.

Biomass energy

Biomass energy has been used since millennia for meeting out growing needs of human beings. The main sources of biomass energy are trees, crops and animal wastes. Biomass contributes over a third of primary energy in India. Biomass fuels are mainly used in rural areas in households for cooking foods and water heating, as well as by traditional and artisan industries. Biomass delivers most of the energy for the domestic use, for example, in rural areas it is about 90% and urban is 40% in India.

However, most of the biomass energy in India is derived from owned sources like farm trees or cattle, or it is collected by households from common property lands. The biomass energy consumption is primarily limited to meet food cooking needs of households and traditional rural industries and services in village areas. However, in absence of established energy market in rural areas, most biomass fuels are not traded nor do they compete with commercial energy resources. With the availability of this energy in plenty, in developing countries, biomass does not acquire resource value so long as it is not scarce. In the absence of an energy market in India, the traditional biomass fails to acquire exchange value in substitution. Absence of market thus acts as a barrier to the penetration of efficient and clean energy resources and technologies.

Biomass energy includes solid biomass like, organic, i.e., non-fossil material of biological origins; biogas, i.e., principally methane and carbon dioxide produced by anaerobic digestion of biomass and combusted to produce heat and/or power; liquid bio-fuels, i.e., bio-based liquid fuel from biomass transformation, mainly used in transportation applications, and municipal waste, i.e., wastes produced by the residential, commercial and public services sectors and incinerated in specific installations to produce heat and/or power.

Biomass Energy

In India, the most successful forms of biomass are sugarcane bagasse in agriculture, pulp and paper residues in forestry and cow-dung and manure in livestock residues. However, it is argued that biomass can directly substitute fossil fuels, as more effective in reducing the atmospheric CO^2 than carbon sequestration in trees. The Kyoto Protocol further encourages the use of biomass energy.

Biomass may be used in a number of ways to produce energy. The most common methods are:

- Combustion.
- Gasification.
- Fermentation.
- Anaerobic digestion.

India is very rich in biomass. It has a potential of 19,500 MW (3,500 MW from bagasse based cogeneration and 16,000 MW from surplus biomass). Currently, India has 537 MW commissioned and 536 MW under construction. The facts reinforce the idea of a commitment by India to develop these resources of power production.

Following is a list of some States with most potential for biomass production:

- Andhra Pradesh (200 MW)
- Bihar (200 MW)
- Gujarat (200 MW)
- Karnataka (300 MW)
- Maharashtra (1,000 MW)
- Punjab (150 MW)
- Tamil Nadu (350 MW)
- Uttar Pradesh (1,000 MW)

Biomass based electric power generation technologies have however, succeeded in nook applications such as supplying electricity in decentralised location and industries generating biomass waste. The large-scale piercing of biomass power technologies depends on their delivered cost and reliability in direct competition with conventional forms of electricity resources in centralised electricity supply. In India, the dominant competing source for electricity supply is the coal-based power.

However, there is variation in biomass energy cost, depending upon the source, location etc. Delivered cost of coal also varies depending upon the extraction costs and logistic costs which vary with the increasing distance from the mine. Coal power plants are built with large scale technology, with a standard size of 500 MW. Scale of grid-based biomass plants vary from a 1 MW to 50 MW.

The use of Biomass energy is growing globally. Despite significant advancements in biomass energy technologies, most Bio-energy consumption in India still remains concentrated and confined to traditional uses. The modern technologies offer possibilities to convert biomass into synthetic gaseous or liquid fuels (like ethanol and methanol) and electricity. Lack of biomass energy market has been the primary barrier to the penetration of modern biomass technologies. Growing experience with modern biomass technologies in India suggests that technology push policies need to be substituted or augmented by market pull policies.

There is large biomass use in India. The bio-energy is confined primarily to traditional uses such as cooking in rural households and heating in rural industries. Most biomass is not traded on the market, but is gathered or homegrown for own use by family labour. The key policy issue is to develop market for biomass energy service. A primary response is to modernise the biomass use. Lately, there has been a growing experience of modern biomass technologies in India. The penetrations of modern biomass energy services at present remain insignificant. The approach to penetrate biomass technologies through government programmes push. Due to high cost and low service reliability, the biomass energy is not yet competitive to cause significant demand (market) pull. Biomass is however competitive in niche applications such as in remote biomass rich locations and agro and wood processing industries generating cheaply available biomass waste. Biomass penetration is also hampered by implicit environmental subsidy enjoyed by fossil fuels.

A primary policy hampering the growth of modern biomass energy is the implicit environmental subsidy allowed to fossil fuels. Increasing realisation among policy-makers about positive externalities of biomass has now created conditions for biomass to make inroads into the energy market.

The bio-energy sector in India is currently driven by Government of India's initiatives. Key government ministries such as Ministry of New and Renewable Energy (MNRE), Ministry of Environment and Forests (MoEF) have had a significant role in promotion of bio-energy. The experimentation on bio-energy plantation is currently being experimented as an approved task under India's flagship programme of national employment generation scheme. The Planning Commission of India has taken major interest in promotion of bio-energy in its programme, Integrated Energy Policy 2003. A diagrammatic overview of the role of stakeholders is presented in the figure below.

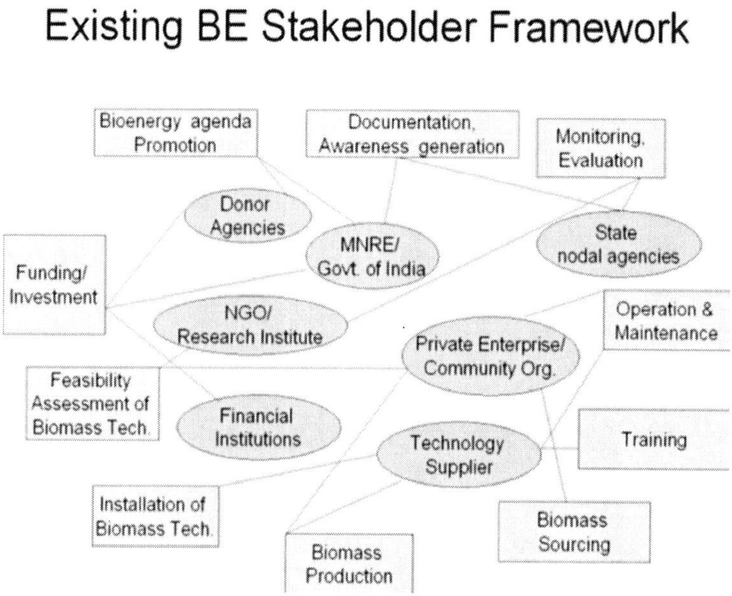

Tidal and Wave energy

Tidal energy is also considered as a renewable energy source, because tides are caused by the orbital mechanics of the solar system and are considered inexhaustible within the human timeframe. Tidal energy is also a form of pollution free energy, which has a lot of potential to be exploited. Though these potentials have not been fully utilised yet, we can't deny the advantage of such kind of a renewable energy.

Tidal power is one of the oldest forms of energy that are used by human beings. However, the use of tide mills, on the Spanish, French and British coasts, date back to 787 AD but it is likely that there were predecessors lost in the anonymity of prehistory. The tide mills consist of a storage pond, filled by the incoming flood water, tied through a sluice and emptied during the outgoing (ebb) tide through a water wheel. The tides turned waterwheels, producing mechanical power to mill grain and power was available for about two to three hours, usually twice a day.

Tidal Energy

The requirement of the growing energy demands by the developed industrial countries dwarf the output of the early tidal barrages. It was not until the 1960's that for the first time commercial-scale modern-era tidal power plant was installed, near St. Malo, France. The hydro mechanical devices such as the paddlewheel and the overshot waterwheel have given way to highly-efficient bulb-type hydroelectric turbine/generator sets. This tidal barrage uses twenty-four 10 MW low-head bulb-type turbine generator sets. Installed in 1965, the barrage has been functioning without missing a tide for more than 45 years.

However, the first tidal power plant with an average tidal range of 8 meters was completed at the mouth of the La Rance estuary on the Brittany coast of France in 1966. Having a capacity of 240 MW, this plant has been working successfully ever since and meets the needs of the equivalent of a city of 300,000 people.

Tidal Power Plant

Tides are caused mainly by the gravitational attraction of the moon on the world's oceans. The sun also plays a significant role, not through its radiant energy but in the form of its gravitational pull, which exerts small additional effect on tidal rhythms. And the rotation of the earth is also a factor in the production of tides.

Tidal cycles are calculated by using harmonic constants defined by having a regular pattern of movements of the sun, moon, and earth. The earth is spinning, pulsating and working together with its celestial neighbours in an ever-changing and infinite series of movements that causes the oceans to rise and fall. These complex patterns have been closely observed for eons and are now known and mathematically predictable, down to the finest detail across the broadest framework of time. However, it is possible to know the precise and specific tidal

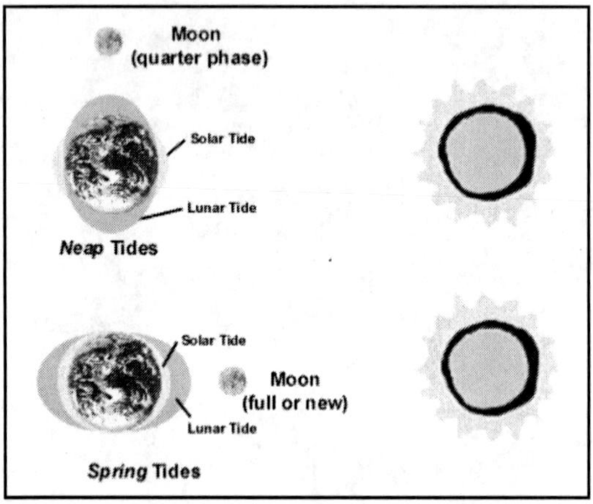

http://wwwphys.murdoch.edu.au/rise/reslab/resfiles/tidal)

level at a specific location at a specific moment of 100 or 1000 years in the future. Wind and weather cause changes under extreme conditions like 'tidal surges', and these events are not accurately predictable, but the basic harmonic changes in water levels caused by the tides are eminently predictable.

However, on a global level, the tides are meters high bulge in the level of the ocean that moves across the globe every 24 hours and 50 minutes. As this bulge nears land, it is changed in amplitude by the decreasing depth and anomalies of the seabed. On the other side at the extremes, some tidal ranges are as small as 6 inches and some are as large as 60 feet. Broad-mouthed estuaries create the largest tidal ranges and long straight coastlines tend to have the smallest. The availability of power in per unit area in any specific location is a function of the square of the tidal range and thus the largest tidal ranges are the most attractive areas for tidal power generation. The amount of water available in an offshore tidal power generator is a function of the area of seabed impounded. It is most economically viable to build an impoundment structure in a shallow area, so that it follows the most attractive sites for offshore tidal power generation which are for those where the tidal range is high and there are broad tidal flats at minimal depth.

The rise and fall of the sea level can provide energy to electric-generating equipment. The gearing of the equipment is tremendous to turn the very slow motion of the tide into enough displacement to generate energy. Tidal barrages which are built across the suitable estuaries are designed to extract energy from the rise and fall of the tides, using turbines which are located in water passages in the barrages. The potential tidal energy, due to the difference in water levels across the barrages, is converted into kinetic energy in the form of fast running water passing through the turbines. This, in turn, is converted into rotational kinetic energy by the attached blades of the turbine, the spinning turbine then driving a generator to generate electricity. The diagram demonstrates power generation cycle of a tidal power.

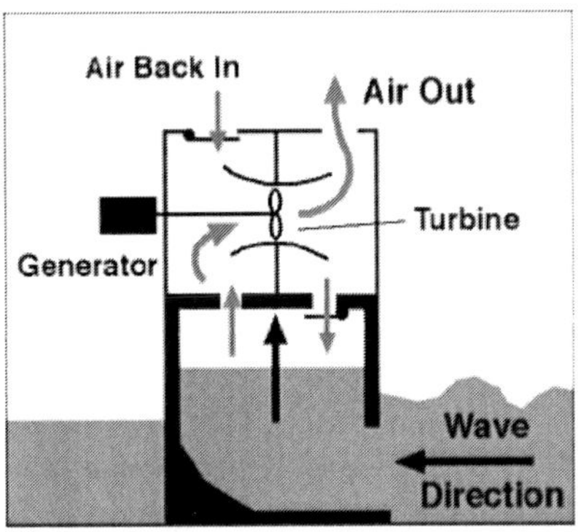

(http://home.clara.net/darvill/altenerg/tidal.htm#intro)

Advantages of tidal power energy:

1. A source of renewable energy needs no fuel to maintain, and thus it is free of charge.
2. Totally no pollution, unlike fossil fuels, it produces no greenhouse gases or other wastes.
3. Predictable source of energy (compared with wind and solar), it is independent of weather and climate change and follows the predictable relationship of the lunar orbit.
4. More efficient than the wind mills because of the density of water.

5. It will protect a large stretch of coastline against damage from high storm tides.

Disadvantages of tidal power energy:

1. Presently it is very costly and expensive to build and maintain (A 1085 MW facility could cost about 1.2 billion dollars to construct and run).
2. Barrage has environmental affects
   (a) Fish and plant migration
   (b) Silt and mud deposits
   (c) Waste and sewage blocks
3. Technology is not fully developed
4. It can provide power only for around 10 hours each day, when the tide is actually moving in or out.

Geothermal energy

Among the various new and renewable energy sources, geothermal energy is known to be one of the clean energies without smoke and also without environmental hazards. Geothermal energy is used to indicate that part of the Earth's heat contained within the Earth that generates geological phenomena on a planetary scale.

The geothermal energy is the energy of the Earth and therefore it is immense, but only a fraction of it could be utilised by mankind. So far, our utilisation of this energy has been limited to areas in which geological conditions permit a carrier i.e., water in the liquid phase or steam, to transfer the heat from deep hot zones to or near the earth surface, thus giving rise to geothermal resources. Innovation and advancement in technological development in the near future, however, may offer new perspectives in this sector.

However, the exploitation of the natural steam for its mechanical energy began at much the same time. The geothermal steam was first used to raise liquids in primitive gas lifts and later in reciprocating and centrifugal pumps and winches, all of these were used in drilling or the local boric acid chemical industry.

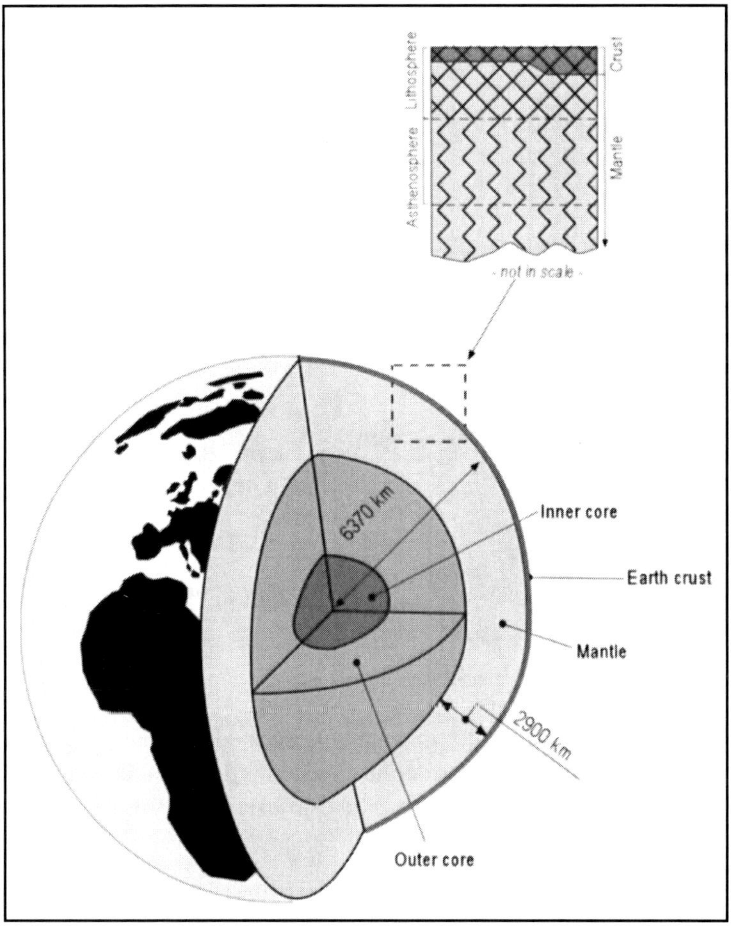

Earth's Structure

During the 20th century, the geothermal energy has been utilised on a large scale for space-heating, industrial use and electricity generation, especially in the countries like, Iceland, Japan and New Zealand.

Geothermal energy is almost as cheap as hydro-energy and will thus be increasingly utilised in the future. However, water from geothermal reservoirs often contains minerals that are corrosive and polluting. In addition, geothermal fluids are a growing problem which must be treated before disposal.

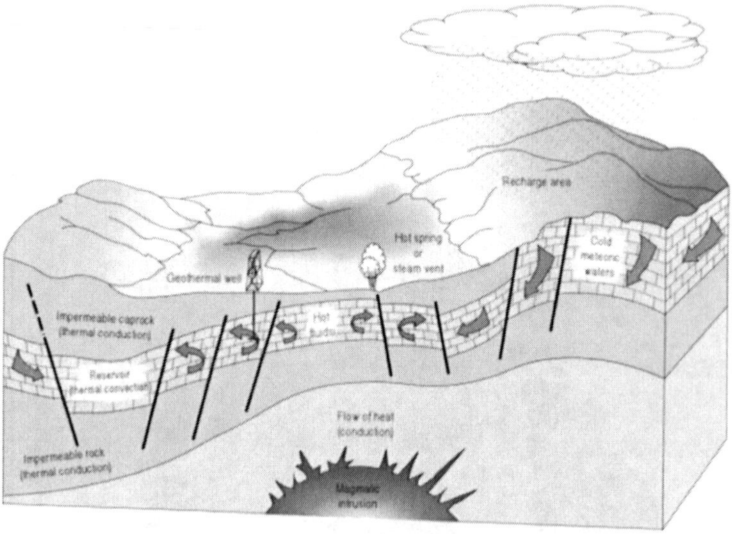

(Schematic representation of an ideal geothermal system)

As geothermal energy is usually described as *renewable* and *sustainable*, it is important to define these terms. Renewable describes a property of the energy source, whereas sustainable describes how the resource is utilised.

The most critical factor for the classification of geothermal energy as a renewable energy source is the rate of energy recharge. In the exploitation of natural geothermal systems, energy recharge takes place by advection of thermal water on the same time scale as production from the resource. This is however, justified the classification of geothermal energy as a renewable and sustainable energy resource. In the case of hot, dry rocks, and some of the hot water aquifers in sedimentary basins, energy recharge is only by thermal conduction; due to the slow rate of the latter process, however, hot dry rocks and some sedimentary reservoirs should be considered as finite energy resources.

Relationship between Environment and Development

Development and environment are interrelated to each other. Improper or uncontrolled development is likely to cause harmful impacts on the natural environment, and environmental pollution or environmental degradation may become a major problem for social and economic development.

The interrelationship between development and environment has been observed throughout the world, especially in fast-developing country like India.

By the end of the 1960s, the attention for environmental concern was heard almost uniquely in the countries of the western world. In the communist world, the relentless destruction of the environment in the name of development and industrialisation continued unabated. In developing countries, environmental concerns were regarded as Western luxuries. 'Poverty is the worst form of environmental pollution,' held by India's then Prime Minister, Indira Gandhi, who played a major role in orienting the agenda of the UN Conference on the Human Environment, which was held in Stockholm in 1972, towards the concerns of the developing countries.

Principles of the Stockholm Declaration

1. Human rights must be respected, apartheid and colonialism condemned.
2. Natural resources must be safeguarded.
3. The capacity of the earth to produce renewable resources must be preserved and maintained.
4. Wildlife must be safeguarded.
5. Non-renewable resources must be shared and not over exhausted.
6. Environmental pollution must not exceed the natural environment's capacity to clean itself.
7. Damaging oceanic pollution must be prevented.
8. Development is needed to improve the environment.
9. Developing countries therefore need assistance.

10. Developing countries need reasonable prices for exports to carry out environmental management.
11. Environment policy must not hinder development.
12. Developing countries need money to develop environmental safeguards.
13. Integrated development planning is needed.
14. Rational planning should resolve conflicts between environment and development.
15. Human settlements must be planned to eliminate environmental problems.
16. Governments should plan and adapt their own proper population policies.
17. National institutions must plan for the development of available states natural resources.
18. Science and technology must be used to improve the environment.
19. Environmental education is essential.
20. Environmental research must be promoted, particularly in developing countries.
21. States may exploit their resources as they wish but must not endanger others.
22. Compensation is endangered due to states.
23. Each nation must establish its own standards.
24. There must be cooperation on international issues.
25. International organisations should help to improve the environment.
26. Elimination of mass destruction weapon.

This conference also established the United Nations Environment Programme as the environmental conscience of the UN system. It is easy to claim that most of the major environmental milestones of the 1970s were followed directly from Stockholm. It is important to recognize that Stockholm was itself a reflection of the changing taste and mood of the times, or at least of the views of many in the West that said it is still instructive to itemize some of the major changes that followed Stockholm.

Also, the Stockholm Conference recommended creating a small secretariat in the United Nations as a focal point for environmental action and coordination within the UN system and this was established later in 1972 under the name of the United Nations Environment Programme (UNEP), and was chaired by an executive director whose responsibilities include:

- To provide support to UNEP's Governing Council.
- To coordinate environmental programmes within the United Nations system.
- To advise on the formulation and implementation of environmental programmes.
- To secure the cooperation of scientific and other professional communities from all over the world.
- To advise on international cooperation in the field of the environment.
- To submit the proposals on medium and long-term planning for United Nations programmes in the environment field.

Today, UNEP mission is working to provide leadership and encourage partnership in caring for the environment by inspiring, informing, and enabling nations and people to improve their quality of life without compromising the nature of future generations.

However, communicating the message that environment and development were interdependent required a process which carried authority and credibility to the North and South, to government and the business sector, to international organisations and civil society. The World Commission on Environment and Development (WCED), which is also known as the **'Brundtland Commission'**, was formed in 1983 to hold hearings across the globe and produce a formal report of its findings. The report was issued after three years of hearings and discussions with the government leaders and the public worldwide on environment and development issues. Public meetings were held in both developed and developing countries, and the process empowered different groups to articulate their views related with the issues like, agriculture, forestry, water, energy, technology transfer and sustainable development in general. *Our Common Future*, the Commission's final report, defined sustainable development as 'development that meets the needs of the present without compromising the ability of future generations to meet their own needs', making it part of the environment lexicon. Thus, sustainable development is also becoming a scientific and technological endeavour that, according to the Initiative on Science and Technology for Sustainable Development it seeks to enhance the contribution of knowledge to environmentally sustainable human development around the world.

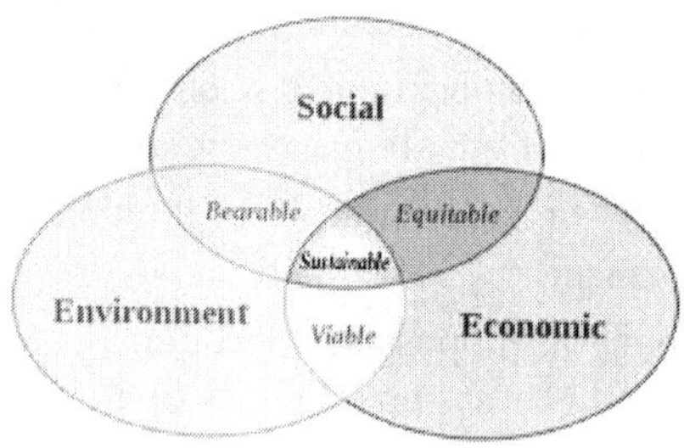

Sustainable Development

This is however, an emerging enterprise which is focused on deepening our understanding of socio-ecological systems in particular places while exploring innovative mechanisms for producing knowledge so that it is relevant, credible, and legitimate to local decision makers.

The efforts of the science and technology community to contribute to sustainable development is exemplified in the actions of the major Academies of Science and International Disciplinary Unions, in collaborative networks of individual scientists and technologists, in emerging programmes of interdisciplinary education, and in many efforts to supply scientific support to communities.

One of the successes of sustainable development has been the ability of it to serve as a grand compromise between those who are principally concerned with nature and environment, those who value economic development, and those who are dedicated to improve the human condition and human welfare. At the core of this compromise is the inseparability of environment and development described by the World Commission on Environment and Development. Thus, much of what is described as sustainable development in practice are negotiations in which workable compromises are found that address the environmental, economic, and human development objectives of competing various interest groups. Indeed, this is why there are so many definitions of sustainable development include statements about open and democratic decision making.

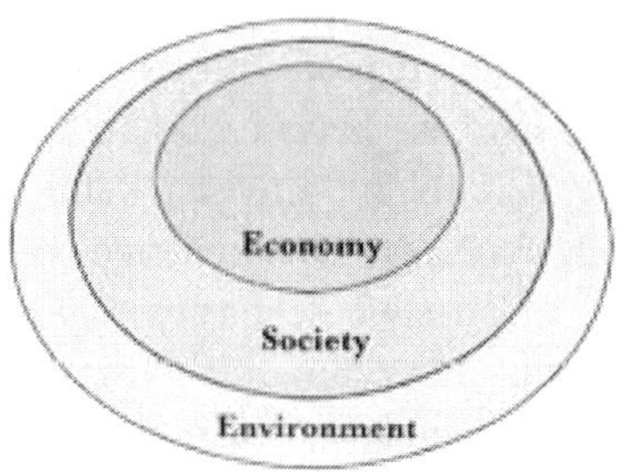

The Commission highlighted environmental problems such as global warming and ozone layer depletion that were new at the time. It expressed concern that the rate of 'change is outstripping the ability of scientific disciplines and our current capabilities to assess and advise'. The Commission concluded that the structure of existing decision-making process and institutional arrangements, both at international and national level, simply could not cope with the demands of sustainable development (WCED 1987).

Global warming, the phenomenon of increasing average air temperatures near the surface of Earth over the past one to two centuries. Climate scientists have since the mid-20th century gathered detailed observations of various weather phenomena (such as temperatures, precipitation, and storms) and of related influences on climate (such as ocean currents and the atmosphere's chemical composition). These data indicate that Earth's climate has changed over almost every conceivable timescale since the beginning of geologic time and that the influence of human activities since at least the beginning of the Industrial Revolution has been deeply woven into the very fabric of climate change. To study the impact of global warming, Intergovernmental Panel on Climate Change (IPCC) was formed in 1988 by the World Meteorological Organisation (WMO) and the United Nations Environment Programme (UNEP).

IPCC, in 2018 produced a special report noting that human beings and human activities have been responsible for a worldwide average temperature increase of between 0.8 and 1.2°C (1.4 and 2.2°F) of global warming since preindustrial times, and most of the warming observed over the second half of the 20th century could be attributed to human activities. Report predicted that the global mean surface temperature would increase between 3 and 4°C (5.4 and 7.2°F) by 2100 relative to the 1986–2005 average should carbon emissions continue at their current rate. The predicted rise in temperature was based on a range of possible scenarios that accounted for future greenhouse gas emissions and mitigation (severity reduction) measures and on uncertainties in the model projections. Some of the main uncertainties include the precise role of feedback processes and the impacts of industrial pollutants known as aerosols, which may offset some warming.

Scientists are agreed that significant societal, economic, and ecological damage would result if global average temperatures rose by more than 2°C (3.6°F) in such a short time. Such damage would include increased extinction of many plant and animal species, shifts in patterns of agriculture, and rising sea levels.

Environment and sustainable development became popular subjects of study in more of the established social and natural sciences, but also new disciplines were born to address cross-cutting areas.

Environmental economics, environmental engineering and other previously fringe subjects started to become established and legitimate fields of scholarship, developing their own theories but also proving their worth in real world contexts.

The environmental sustainability, however, did not feature high in the principles and particularly practice of bilateral aid. As an early sign of change, in 1987 the OECD established a Development Advisory Committee charged with the establishment of guidelines for the integration of environment and sustainable development in development assistance programmes.

The successful outcomes of the Montreal Protocol in 1987 were held as a promising model for cooperation between North hemisphere and South hemisphere, government and business to address the concern related with global environmental matters. However, dealing with ozone depletion was more straightforward than dealing with other environmental issues that entered the public agenda in the 1980s, like, climate change.

The Intergovernmental Panel on Climate Change

The Intergovernmental Panel on Climate Change (IPCC) was established in 1988 with three working groups focused on the scientific assessment of climate change, environmental and socio-economic impacts, and response strategies, foretelling the wide range of challenges that humanity would face as it entered the last decade of the millennium. The establishment of the IPCC by UNEP and the World Meteorological Organisation (WMO) helped develop a broad consensus on the science, social impacts and best responses to human-induced global warming. The IPCC has contributed enormously to create public understanding of the dangers of global warming, particularly in advance industrialised countries. In many developing countries, where the studies on climate change are rare and climate experts almost non-existent, climate change is not regarded in the same light. This has also led some organisations in the developing regions to complain about 'an enormous disparity in North-South participation'. It argues that Southern countries have no coordinated national climate programmes, few climate researchers, and hardly any data to compute long-term climate projections.

Source: UNEP, Abdel Saurad-Mali, Kuwait, TophamPicturePoint

Firemen trying to extinguish a burning oil rig in Kuwait in 1991

Recognizing detrimental effects of environmental pollution and degradation on sustainable development, the United Nations Conference on Environment and Development, which was held from June 3 to June 14, 1992 in Rio de Janeiro, Brazil discussed and agreed on several global environmental issues including non-binding statements on the relationship between sustainable environmental practices and the pursuit of social and socioeconomic development.

The Summit produced at least seven major achievements:

- The Rio de Janeiro Declaration on Environment and Development contains 27 principles.
- *Agenda 21*- a blueprint for environment and development into the 21st century.
- Two major international conventions, like, the United Nations Framework Convention on Climate Change (UNFCCC) and the Convention on Biological Diversity (CBD).

- The Commission on Sustainable Development.
- General agreement to negotiate a world desertification convention.
- The Principle statement for the Sustainable Management of Forests.

Agenda 21 stresses for a solid foundation of the promotion of sustainable development in terms of social, economic and environmental progress. *Agenda 21* has 40 chapters, and its recommendations are mainly divided into four areas:

- Social and economic issues such as international cooperation to accelerate sustainable development, combating poverty, changing consumption patterns, demographic dynamics and sustainability, and protecting and promoting human health.
- Conservation and management of natural resources for sustainable development, such as preservation and protection of the atmosphere, combating deforestation, combating desertification and drought, promoting sustainable agriculture and rural development, conservation of biological diversity, protection of freshwater resources and the oceans, and the proper management of toxic chemicals and hazardous wastes.
- Strengthening the key role of major groups like, women, children and youth, indigenous people and their communities, NGOs, local authorities' initiatives in support of *Agenda 21*, workers and their trade unions, business and industry, the scientific and technological community, and farmers.
- Means of implementation, including financial resources and mechanisms, transfer of environmentally sound technology, promoting education, public awareness and training, international institutional arrangements, international legal instruments and mechanisms, and information for decision-making.

The principle of Rio de Janeiro declarations reaffirmed the issues that had been articulated in Stockholm 20 years earlier, placing human beings at the centre of sustainable development concerns by stating that humans are entitled to a healthy and productive life in harmony with nature.

However, the Earth Summit provides a forum to address issues of both environment and development, and to highlight differences in perspective between the North hemisphere and South hemisphere. After the Earth Summit, sustainable development took on a life of its own, forcing its way into the deliberations of bodies ranging from city councils to international organisations. More than 150 countries have established national-level institutions to develop an integrated approach to sustainable development- although, in some countries, the national councils of sustainable development have been more of a political view than substantive in nature.

The main goal of the UNFCCC is to stabilise the emissions of the greenhouse gases at levels that will prevent dangerous anthropogenic interference with the global climate. The common principle and differentiated responsibilities which were embraced by this convention has guided the adoption of a regulatory structure. This principle showed the reality that most emissions of greenhouse gases are from industrialised states. The Kyoto Protocol, which aims for emissions reductions, was opened for signature in 1997. As of December 2001, 84 Parties had signed and 46 Parties had ratified or acceded to the Protocol (UNFCCC 2001). A notable exception was the United States which announced its decision not to ratify the Protocol in early 2001.

According to the 'The Indian Express' on 9 August 2021, The IPCC is now saying that the rise in global temperatures was a direct result of human activities. In the previous assessment reports, the IPCC had said that human activities were "likely", or "most likely" behind the rising temperatures. The latest report says it was "unequivocal" that this was indeed the case. Further going into the detailed study of the report, it also reveals that the 2°C warming is likely to get exceeded by the end of this century unless immediate and deep reductions in greenhouse gas emissions are initiated immediately. What gets masked in this statement is the fact that in the business-as-usual, or worst-case, scenario, the temperature rise by the end of the century would exceed even 4°C.

According to 'The Hindu' newspaper editorial on 10 August 2021, has issued arguably its strongest warning yet on impending catastrophe from unmitigated global warming caused by human activity, lending scientific credence to the argument that rising wildfires, heatwaves, extreme rainfall and floods witnessed in recent times are all strongly influenced by a changing climate. In a stark report on the physical science basis of climate change contributed for a broader Assessment Report of the UN, the IPCC's Working Group-I has called for deep cuts to carbon dioxide emissions and other greenhouse gases and a move to net zero emissions, as the world would otherwise exceed 1.5°C and 2°C of warming during the 21st century with permanent consequences. Climate change is described by many as a far greater threat to humanity than COVID-19, because of its irreversible impacts. The latest report is bound to strengthen the criticism that leaders in many countries have stonewalled and avoided moving away from coal and other fossil fuels, while even those who promised to act, failed to influence the multilateral system. The new report attributes catastrophic events to sustained global warming, particularly the frequency and intensity of hot extremes, marine heatwaves, heavy precipitation, agricultural and ecological droughts, proportion of intense tropical cyclones, reductions in Arctic Sea ice, snow cover and permafrost. A phenomenon such as heavy rainfall over land, for instance, could be 10.5% wetter in a world warmer by 1.5°C, and occur 1.5 times more often, compared to the 1850-1900 period.

The Convention on Biological Diversity

The Convention on Biological Diversity came into scene in 1993. The Convention on Biological Diversity is an international treaty for the conservation of biodiversity, the sustainable use of the components of biodiversity and the equitable sharing of the benefits derived from the use of genetic resources. This was the first global agreement on the conservation and sustainable use of biodiversity which serves as a blueprint for national action. This Convention establishes three major goals, i.e., the conservation of biological diversity, the sustainable use of its components, and the fair and equitable sharing of the benefits from the use of genetic natural resources. This convention addresses many biodiversity issues like, habitat preservation, intellectual property rights, bio-safety and indigenous peoples' rights. The Convention marks a landmark in the international law, noted for its comprehensive and ecosystems approach to protect biodiversity. The treaty has gained rapid and widespread acceptance. By the end of 2001AD, a total of 182 governments had ratified the agreement. A supplementary agreement to the Convention, the Cartagena Protocol on Bio-safety, was adopted in January 2000 to address the potential risks posed by cross-border trade and accidental releases of living genetically modified organisms. The adoption of the bio-safety protocol is a major success for developing countries of which it was called for. Till 2001, this protocol was signed by 103 parties and ratified by 9 parties. The CBD has also influenced the enactment of a law which seeks to regulate genetic resources within the Andean Pact nations of Bolivia, Colombia, Ecuador, Peru and Venezuela. The law became effective in July 1996.

The Cartagena Protocol on Biosafety and the Nagoya Protocol on Access and Benefit Sharing are supplementary agreements to the Convention. The Cartagena Protocol, which entered into force on 11 September 2003, seeks to protect biological diversity from the potential risks posed by living modified organisms resulting from

Biodiversity

modern biotechnology. To date, 173 Parties have ratified the Cartagena Protocol. Brazil, the most biodiverse country in the world, on 4 March 2021 ratified the Nagoya Protocol on access to genetic resources and the fair and equitable way, including by appropriate access to genetic resources and by appropriate transfer of relevant technologies. It entered into force on 12 October 2014 and to date has been ratified by 130 Parties.

In essence, environment is the land, air and water around us, basically sustaining life as we know it. Mankind and all other life systems evolved over the ages. While we may, yet, not have a complete understanding of the complex processes through which evolution has occurred.

However, it is indisputable that human is the final product of this environment. On earth, this process of change is incessant. The very fact of its existence is that the living beings do influence their nature and get influenced by the environment around them. Man, like other plant or animal species, does the same. However, the present concern for environmental conservation and preservation arises from the impact of human actions on the environment on a scale fundamentally different from what has been witnessed before.

Till now, we have realised that how important it is to protect the environment for our own survival. The term 'conservation' of natural environment relates to activities which can provide individual or commercial benefits, but at the same time, prevent its overuse leading to environmental damage. Conservation may be differentiated from preservation, which is considered to be 'maintaining of nature as it is, or might have been before the intervention of either human beings or natural forces'. We all know that natural resources are getting depleted and environmental problems are increasing at a greater pace. With the increasing advancement in technologies and human desires for luxurious good there is a tremendous pressure over the existing resources. To this development it is important to utilise the available resources in sustainable manner so that the need of the future generation can also be fulfilled. Thus, sustainable development is the need of the hour. With the increasing demand of the energy to drive life it is very important to have an alternative source of energy that is not conventional like, coal, petroleum, gas etc. but the non-conventional energy like, solar, wind, hydro, biogas, biomass, geothermal energy etc. These non-conventional energies are non-polluted and available in abundant in the nature. Thus, with the help of advanced technologies we can harness this energy and fulfill our desire without disturbing the environment.

Chapter - 3

Environmental Degradation

Environmental degradation can be understood as a result of the dynamic inter-play of socio-economic, institutional and technological activities. Environmental changes may be driven by many factors including economic growth, population growth, urbanisation, intensification of agriculture, rising energy use and transportation. Poverty still remains a problem as the root cause of several environmental problems. Due to uncontrolled urbanisation in India, environmental degradation has been occurring very rapidly and causing shortages of housing, polluting water quality, excessive air pollution, noise pollution, dust and heat, and the problems of disposal of solid wastes and hazardous wastes. The large and metropolitan cities present a particularly depressing picture today.

Environmental Degradation

The key environmental challenges that a country faces are related to the nexus of environmental degradation with poverty in its various dimensions, and economic growth. These challenges are however, intrinsically related to the state of environmental natural resources, such as land, water, air, and their flora and fauna. The main causes of environmental degradation are population growth, inappropriate technology and consumption choices, and poverty, leading to changes in relations between people and ecosystems, and development activities such as intensive agriculture, polluting industry, and unplanned urbanisation. However, these factors give rise to environmental degradation only through deeper causal linkages, in particular, institutional failures, resulting in the lack of clarity or enforcement of rights of access and use of natural environmental resources and policies which provide disincentives for environmental conservation and which may have origins in the fiscal regime, and market failures which may be linked to shortcomings in the regulatory regimes, and governance constraints.

Environmental degradation is one of the major causal factors in enhancing and perpetuating poverty, particularly among the poor of rural areas when such environmental degradation impacts on soil fertility, quantity and quality of water, air quality, forests, wildlife and fisheries. The dependence of the rural poor, in particular, tribal societies, on their natural resources and especially on biodiversity, is self-evident.

It is evidenced that women in particular face much adverse impacts of degradation of natural resources which are directly responsible for their collection and use, but rarely for their management. The commitment of time and effort in collection of these resources has a direct impact on the capacity of rural women to give time to raising and educating children, enhancing their earning skills, or participating in useful livelihoods. Poverty, however, can itself accentuate environmental degradation, given that institutional failures persist.

Several environmental resources are complementary in production and consumption to other commodities, like, water in relation to agricultural production, fuel wood in relation to consumption of food, while a number of environmental resources are a source of income or food, like, fisheries, non-timber forest produce, for the poor. This is a common source of cumulative causation, where poverty, gender inequalities, and environmental degradation mutually reinforce each other. Poverty and environmental degradation are also reinforced by the population growth, which in turn, depends on a complex interaction of diverse causal factors and stages of development. The social and economic context of population growth has been detailed in the National Population Policy 2000, which recognizes stabilisation of population as a necessary condition for sustainable development.

Causes of Environmental Degradation

Social Factors

Population: Population is one of the important sources of development, yet it is also a major source of environmental degradation when it exceeds the optimum level of the support systems. Unless the relationship between the increasing population and the life support system can be stabilised, development programmes are not likely to yield desired results.

The impact of population on the environment is primarily through the use of natural resources and production of wastes. It is also associated with environmental stresses like loss of biodiversity, air and water pollution and increased pressure on arable land.

According to the latest United Nations data 2021, India supports around 17.7 percent of the world population on just 2.4 percent of world land area. Its current rate of population growth at 1.85 percent continues to pose a persistent population challenge on environment. In view of the linkages between population and environment, a vigorous drive for population control need hardly be over emphasised.

Poverty: Poverty poses both cause and effect on environmental degradation. The circular link between poverty and environment is an intricate complex phenomenon. Inequality may foster un-sustainability because the poor, who depend on natural resources are more than the rich, deplete natural resources faster as they have no real prospects of gaining access to other types of resources. Moreover, degraded environment can accelerate the process of impoverishment, again because the poor depend directly on natural resource assets. Although there has been a significant decline in the poverty ratio in the country from 55% in 1973 to 36% in 1993-94 and the absolute number of poor have, however, remained constant at around 320 million over the years. Acceleration in poverty alleviation programmes is imperative to break this link between poverty and the environment.

Urbanisation: Lack of opportunities for gainful employment in villages and the ecological stresses is leading to an ever-increasing movement of poor families to towns. Mega cities are emerging and urban slums are expanding. There has been a huge increase in urban population over 1901-1991. During the past two decades of 1971-91, India's urban population has doubled from 109 million to 218 million and is estimated to reach 300 million by 2000 AD. However, in 2011 census it was 377.1 million and is projected to 1,380 million or 138 crore people in 2020.

The rapid and unplanned expansion of urban areas has resulted in degradation of urban environment. It has widened the gulf between demand and supply of infrastructural services such as energy, housing, transport, communication, education, water supply and sewage and recreational amenities, thus depleting the precious environmental resource base of the cities. The result is showing that the growing trend in deterioration of air and water quality, generation of urban wastes, the proliferation of slum areas and undesirable land use changes, all of which contribute to urban poverty.

Economic Factors

Environmental degradation, to a large extent is the result of market failure, i.e., the non-existent or poorly functioning markets for environmental goods and services. In this context, environmental degradation is a particular case of consumption or production externalities reflected by divergence between private and social costs or benefits. However, lack of well-defined property rights may be one of the reasons for such market failure. On the other hand, Market distortions created by price controls and subsidies may aggravate the achievement of environmental objectives.

The level and pattern of economic development also affect the nature of environmental problems. India's development objectives have consistently emphasised the promotion of policies and programmes for economic growth and social welfare. Between 1994-95 and 1997-98, the Indian economy has grown a little over 7 percent per annum: the growth of industrial production and manufacturing averaging higher at 8.4 percent and 8.9 percent respectively during these years. The manufacturing technologies adopted by most of the industries have created a heavy pressure on environment especially through intensive resource and energy use, as are evident in natural resource depletion, like, fossil fuel, minerals, timber, water, air and land contamination, health hazards and degradation of natural eco-systems. With high proportion fossil fuel as the main source of industrial energy and major air polluting industries such as iron and steel, fertilisers and cement growing, industrial sources have contributed to a relatively high share in air pollution. Huge quantities of industrial and hazardous wastes brought about by expansion of chemical based industries have compounded the wastes management problem with serious environmental health implications.

Increasing transport activities have a great effect on the natural environment such as air pollution, noise pollution from road traffic and oil spills from marine shipping. Transport infrastructure in India has expanded considerably in terms of network systems and services. Thus, transportation system accounts for a major share of air pollution in cities such as Delhi, Mumbai, Kolkata and Chennai. The impacts of port and harbor projects are mainly on sensitive coastal eco systems. Their construction affects the hydrology system, surface water quality, fisheries, coral reefs and mangroves to a large extent.

However, the direct impacts of agricultural development on the environment arise from agricultural activities which contribute to severe soil erosion, land salinisation and loss of nutrients. The spread of green revolution has been accompanied by over exploitation of soil fertility and water resources, and use of chemical fertilisers and pesticides have increased many fold. On the other side, shifting cultivation in hilly and forested areas has also been an important cause of land degradation. Leaching from extensive use of pesticides and chemical fertilisers is an important source of contamination of water bodies and thus pollution. Intensive agriculture and irrigation contribute to land degradation particularly salinisation, alkalisation and water logging.

Institutional Factors

The Ministry of Environment & Forests (MOEF) in the Government is responsible for protection, conservation and development of environment. The Ministry works in close collaboration with other Ministries, State Governments, Pollution Control Boards and a number of scientific and technical institutions, universities, non-governmental organisations etc.

Environment Protection Act, 1986 plays the key role in legislation and governing environment management. Other important legislations in the area are the Forest Conservation Act, 1980 and the Wildlife Protection Act, 1972. The weakness of the existing system lies in the enforcement measurements of environmental institutions, both at the centre and the state level.

It has been seen that there is no efficient and effective coordination amongst various Ministries/Institutions regarding integration of environmental concerns at various levels of the inception and planning of the project. Current policies are also fragmented across several Government agencies with differences in policy mandates. Also lack of trained personnel and comprehensive database delay many projects.

Most of the State Government institutions are relatively small and suffering from inadequacy of technical staff and resources. Although overall quality of Environmental Impact Assessment (EIA) studies and the effective implementation of the EIA process have improved over the years; institutional strengthening measures such as training to the key professionals and staffs with proper technical education is needed to make the EIA procedure a more effective instrument for environment protection and sustainable development.

Deforestation

Forests provide various environmental services. Prominent among these is the recharging of mountain aquifers, which sustain our rivers. They also conserve and protect the soil, and prevent floods and drought. Forests provide habitat for wildlife and maintain the ecological conditions for maintenance and natural evolution of genetic diversity of flora and fauna. They are the traditional homes of forest dwelling tribal people, and the major part by far of whose livelihoods depend on forests. They yield forest timber, fuel wood, and other forest produce, and possess great potential for economic benefits, in particular for local communities, from sustainable eco-tourism.

India is a country of various types of relief and structure encompassing a large canvas of habitats, and ecological niches; rich in bio-diversity and simultaneously supporting a rich and vibrant diversity of human cultures.

The environments are as diverse as can be imagined; from the Himalayas in the north, the long coastline touched by the Arabian Sea on the west and the Bay of Bengal in the east to the islands of Andaman and Nicobar and the Lakshadweep.

From the deserts of Rajasthan and Gujarat in the west to the teak forests of Central India to the thick and towering rainforests in the North East large parts of India like most other parts of South Asia and for that matter the rest of the world were till recently covered in thick forests.

With this destruction of the stake in and responsibility for the wellbeing of the forests the people who have lived in and tended the forests for generations were forced to participate in and share the blame for destruction of the forests.

This process of deforestation continues even today in various forms in many parts of the country, resulting in the rapid decline in forest cover.

Increasing deforestation has not only raised the problem of local but also global environmental degradation complications. It can also affect sustainable socio-economic developmental processes in the

Deforestation

various developing countries as forests have been generating a lot of employment opportunities in the primary, secondary and tertiary sectors. Forests have been a source of subsistence to the poorest of the poor in the agricultural economies. Furthermore, inhuman face of deforestation is characterised by the increasing stress on the poorer sections of the society like, women who have been primarily involved in gathering fuel-wood, fodder and water in the traditional village economies.

The scarcity of forest stock in India can be estimated from India's position in the world in terms of population and forest resources. India possesses around 17.7 percent of the world's population and 15 percent of world's livestock, with only 2.4 percent of the world's land area and 1.7 percent of the world's forest stock. Obviously, land and forest resources are not commensurate with the proportionate burden of population and livestock on India's soil.

STATUS OF INDIA'S FORESTS

National Forest Policy of India, 1988 envisages a goal of achieving 33% of geographical area of the country under forest and tree cover. We have seen that over the last 2-3 decades India have witnessed severe loss of forest lives. If we look at the latest forest survey we find that the awareness regarding our environment has slightly increased.

ISFR 2019 is a biennial report published by the Forest Survey of India (FSI) and is the 16th such report published. The calculations are largely based on satellite data. It includes information on forest cover, tree cover, mangrove cover, growing stock inside and outside the forest areas, carbon stock in India's forests, forest types and biodiversity, forest fire monitoring and forest cover in different slopes and altitudes.

According to the FSI 2019 report, the total forest cover of the country is 712,249 square kilometers (21.67 percent of India's total geographical area) slightly up from 708,273 sq. km (21.54 percent) in 2017. The tree cover of the country is 95,027 sq. km (2.89 percent of the total area) again slightly up from 93,815 sq. km. (2.85 percent) in 2017.

As per the report, "forest cover" includes all tree patches which have canopy density more than 10 percent and area of one hectare or more in size, irrespective of their legal status and species composition. The term "Recorded Forest Area" (RFA) is used for lands which have been notified as "forest" under any government Act or rules or recorded as "forest" in the government records.

Area-wise Madhya Pradesh has the largest forest cover in the country followed by Arunachal Pradesh, Chhattisgarh, Odisha and Maharashtra. In terms of forest cover as percentage of total geographical area, the top five States are Mizoram (85.41%), Arunachal Pradesh (79.63%), Meghalaya (76.33%), Manipur (75.46%) and Nagaland (75.31%).

The concentration of mangroves is mainly in West Bengal, Gujarat and the Andaman and Nicobar Islands. However, the extent of open forests, which are mainly degraded forests, depicts the potential availability for recuperation and regeneration of forests in India.

Source: Ministry of Environment, Forest and Climate Change 2019.

Causes of Deforestation

Environmentalists hold the opinion that the main cause for large-scale destruction of the forest areas in India is rooted in the commercially oriented forest use and ownership policies of the British government. These have continued in their essence for several years even in post-independence India. In the recent times it is the new forests policies and programmes of development, rapid industrialisation, urbanisation and growing materialistic consumerism has resulted in the wide-scale destruction of the forests.

However, the increasing population pressure is always the major cause of overexploitation of the natural resources including forestlands. Possibly, poverty, corrupt practices, weak institutions, and wasteful consumption patterns also combine with the population pressure facilitating the depletion and degradation of forest stock having enormous environmental degradation complications.

Those civilisations, which have looked after the forests by using forests resources carefully have prospered, whereas those destroyed the forests, have gradually impoverished. Today, logging and mining activities are serious causes of loss of forests in our country and all over the world. Dams built for hydroelectric power or irrigation have submerged large tracts of forests and have displaced tribal people whose lives are closely knit to the forest. This has become a serious cause of concern in India. Deforestation is a serious issue that most nations of the world face today and India is one of those countries in the list. Deforestation is primarily due to urbanisation and increasing agricultural activities. Most nations that are presently under the scanner for deforestation had immense forest stretch. The need for settlements and development has triggered such a scenario.

India as a developing nation too faces immense issue of deforestation. Nearly 22.8% of forested area is decreasing slowly. These forests are the habitat for most endangered species and animals. There are over 2,300 species including reptiles, birds and mammals.

India is, like the most other forested regions, have thick dense forests followed by rivers like the Yamuna and the Ganga. However, the Indus Valley Civilisation had eventually led the way for deforestation by creating urban centre. Civilisations in and around the rivers led to land reformation. After India got independence in the year 1947, agriculture no longer remained to be the prime occupation. New developments led to new occupations and industrialisation needed to be expanded. The new forests policies often dragged people from these forest lands and deprived them of their sources to survive.

The basic reasons of deforestation are the followings:

(1) *Expansion of Agriculture:* With the increasing demands for agricultural products, more and more forest land is brought under agricultural activities for which forests are destroyed, grasslands ploughed, uneven grounds leveled, marshes drained and even land water is reclaimed. Such an expansion and the destruction of forests are marked with more ecological destruction. In the regions like tropical climate of the world, as much of the mineral material is lodged in the plant biomass, its removal takes away large part of the soil nutrients. The soil becomes infertile and thus is unable to support farming for long duration.

(2) *Shifting Cultivation:* Cultivation of shifting agricultural practice is considered as another cause for deforestation. In fact, shifting cultivation has occurred due to loss of fertility of the soil. In shifting cultivation, a small patch of tropical forests is cleared and vegetation is destroyed and burnt. Crops are grown as long as the soil is fertile for agriculture production, after which the cultivation is abandoned, and cultivation moves on to a fresh patch of land.

The abandoned used land is allowed to lie for long periods during which the new vegetation took place and natural ecosystem was restored. Thus, shifting cultivations worked in harmony with nature. The used soil is unable to regain its productivity before it is put to use again. This causes degradation and erosion of soil and the failure of crops. As crops fail more and more land is cleared from forests to be put to similar over exploitation. The overall result is that green forests are being gradually replaced by barren waste land.

(3) *Fire Wood Collection:* For the majority of rural populations and the people living in small towns and cities of developing countries, the only source of fuel is wood, which is burnt to cook food and provide heat in chilly winter days. The collection of fire wood contributes much to the depletion of tree cover. Denser forests usually produced a lot of fuel material in the form of dead twigs, leaves etc.

However, in densely wooded localities, there is hardly any need of cutting down live trees. But in case of lightly wooded forests, where the pressure of fuel demand is usually higher, a slow thinning of wood lands occurs due to regular foraging of villagers. However, the tree of dead woods is actually manufactured, trees are cut and their barks girdled and live trees became personal and find their way to local markets.

(4) *Timber Harvesting:* A country's prosperity depends on availability of timber resource as an important asset for the same county. Commercialisation of timber wood is found

ready-made way in national as well as international markets. According to a popular view, the natural forests are being exploited logging or felling of forest trees for obtaining timber is an important cause of deforestation.

Live forest trees with thick and straight trunks are loaded and transported to commercial establishments elsewhere to the consumers. However, in this process large tracts of forests are damaged. The profits from timber trade are more enjoyed by governments, large companies or affluent contractors, local people get a tiny share in the benefits while axing their own resource base.

(5) *Extension of Cultivation on Hill Slopes:* Agricultural activities have always been concentrated in the area of plain and floors valleys. However, farming on narrow flat step cut one after another across the slope for which terrace farming is an age-old practice. The ever-rushing human numbers and their necessities have forced many to go up the mountain's slopes for cultivation. As more and more slopes are cleared, cut down plants, steps are carved out and other cultivation is attempted however after a few crops, the crops productivity is declined.

Consequences of Deforestation

Deforestation is one of the India's serious environmental problems of forest degradation. Due to timber extraction and our dependence on fuel-wood, large areas of forestland are being cleared. A large number of poor mainly from rural areas are still totally dependent on wood to cook their meals and heat their homes. We are not being able to plant enough trees at a sufficient rate to support the need for forest timber and fuel-wood.

On the other hand, in past decades, there has been great loss of forest cover. Though there are now clear signs of reversal of this trend. The primary direct cause of forest loss has been the conversion of forest land for agriculture, human settlements, developing infrastructure, and establishment of industry. In addition to this the commercial extraction of fuel-wood, illegal cutting down of trees,

and uncontrolled grazing of cattle, has degraded forests. These causes, however, have their origins in the fact that the natural environmental values provided by forests are not recognised as direct financial benefits by various parties, at least to the extent of exceeding the monetary incomes from alternative uses, including those arising from illegal use.

Since the ancient times, forest dwelling tribes had generally recognised traditional community ownership over the forests, for which, they had strong incentives to use the forests sustainably and to preserve and protect them from encroachers, following the commencement of formal forest laws and institutions in 1865. These tribal rights over forests were effectively extinguished in many parts of the country. Such disempowerment and loss of control of tribe over the forest land has led to the forests becoming open access in nature, leading to their gradual degradation in a classic manifestation of the "*Tragedy of the Commons*", besides leading to perennial conflict between the tribal people and the Governments Forest Department, and constituting a major denial of justice.

It is however, possible that some site-specific non-forest activities may create overall societal benefits significantly exceeding that from the environmental services provided by the particular and specific tract of forest. However, large scale forest cover loss would definitely lead to catastrophic, permanent change in the country's ecological balance, leading to tremendous stress on water resources and soil erosion, with significant loss of agricultural productivity, industrial potential, living conditions of human beings, and the onset of natural disasters such as drought and floods. In any of these cases, the environmental values of converted forests must be restored, as nearly as may be feasible, to the same publics.

Control of Deforestation

The National Forest Policy, 1988, and the Indian Forest Act, as well as the regulations under it, provide a comprehensive basis for forest conservation. However, it is necessary, looking to some of the underlying causes of forest loss, to take some further steps.

These include:

1. Give traditional rights and legal recognition of forest dwelling tribes. This would provide solution to a serious historical injustice and will secure their livelihoods, lessen the possibilities of conflict with the Forest Departments, and provide long-term incentives to the tribals to conserve the forests.
2. In order to increase forest and tree cover to 33% by 2012, formulate an innovative strategy through afforestation of degraded forest land, wastelands, and tree cover on private or revenue land. Key elements of the strategy would include:
    - The inclusion and implementation of the share of multi-stake-holder partnerships by involving the Forest Department, local communities, and investors, with clearly defined obligations and entitlements for each partner, following good governance principles, to derive environmental, livelihood, and financial benefits.
    - Legalisation of restrictions on cultivation of forest species outside notified forests, to enable farmers to undertake social and farm forestry where their returns are more favourable than cropping, and

- Joint Forestry Management (JFM) system is universalisation throughout the country.

3 Focus public investments on enhancing the density of natural forests, mangroves conservation, and universalisation of Joint Forestry Management.

4 Plan an appropriate methodology for reckoning and restoring the environmental values of forests, which are unavoidably diverted to other uses.

5 Planning and Implementing of a "Code of Best Management Practices" for dense natural forests to realise the Objectives and Principles of NEP, 2004.

Thus, the environment conservation requires the participation of multiple stakeholders, who may bring to bear their respective natural environmental resources, competencies, and perspectives, so that the outcomes of partnerships are superior to those of each acting alone. Proper implementation of policy and policy-making agencies of the Government, at Central, State, Municipal, and village panchayat levels; the legislatures and judiciary; the public and private corporate sectors; financial institutions; industry associations; academic and research institutions; independent professionals and experts; the mass media and community based organisations; voluntary organisations like, NGOs and multilateral and bilateral development partners may play an important roles in partnerships for the formulation, implementation, and promotion of measures for environmental conservation.

In order to realise partnerships successful among these diverse actors, it is essential to eschew the confrontational posturing sometimes adopted in the past.

While it is not possible that the interests and perceptions of all stakeholders will coincide on each occasion, nevertheless, it is necessary to realise that progress will be seriously impeded if the motives of other partners are called into question during public discourse. It is also essential that all partnerships are realised through, and are carried out in terms of the principles of good governance, in particular, transparency, accountability, cost effectiveness, and efficiency.

Environment Conservation

A large number of particular and specific themes for partnerships have been identified. A generic classification of some, certainly not exhaustive and possible partnerships are as follows:

(a) Public-Community Partnerships in which public agencies and local communities coordinate and cooperate in the management of a given environmental resource, each partner bringing agreed resources, assuming specified responsibilities, and with defined entitlements, like, Joint Forestry Management.

(b) Public-Private Partnerships in which specified public functions with respect to environmental management are well defined and contracted out competitively to private providers, e.g. monitoring of environmental quality.

(c) Public-Community-Private Partnerships in terms of which the all the partners assume joint and shared responsibility for a particular environmental function, with defined obligations and entitlements for each, with competitive selection of the private sector partner, like, afforestation of degraded forests.

(d) Public-Voluntary Organisation Partnerships which is very much similar to public-private partnerships, in respect of functions in which voluntary organisations may have a comparative advantage over others, the voluntary organisations, in turn, being selected competitively, like, raising environmental awareness.

(e) Public-Private-Voluntary Organisation Partnerships, in which the provision of specified public responsibilities is accomplished on competitive basis by the private sector and the provision is monitored by competitively selected voluntary organisations.

Enhancing environmental awareness at every level is essential to harmonize patterns of individual behaviour with the requirements of environmental conservation. This would lessen the demands placed on the monitoring and enforcement regimes; in fact, large-scale

Picture: Environmental Education

non-compliance would simply overwhelm any feasible regulatory machinery. Awareness relates to the general public, as well as specific sections, like, the youth, urban dwellers, industrial and construction workers, municipal and other public employees, etc. Environmental awareness involves not only internalisation of environmentally responsible behaviour and values, but also enhanced understanding of the impacts of irresponsible destructive actions, including the public health, living conditions, and livelihood prospects.

Thus, environmental education is the dominant means of enhancing such awareness, both among the public at large, and among focused groups.

Such education may be formal, or informal, or a combination of both. It may rely on educational institutions at different levels; the print, electronic, or live media; and various other formal and informal settings.

Depletion of Water Resources

The total availability of water on the earth has been estimated at 1.4 billion cubic kilometers which is enough to cover the planet with a layer of about 3-km deep. Almost 95% of the earth's water is stored in the oceans, which is useless for human consumption because of its high salt content. About 4% of total water is locked in the polar ice caps and the remaining 1% constitutes all the fresh water in hydrological cycle including ground water reserves. Only 0.1% is available as fresh water in rivers, lakes, and streams, which is potable and suitable for human consumption. This data highlights the significance of the need to preserve and conserve our fresh water resources.

The annual precipitation of rainfall over India is 400 million-hectare meters. The surface water resources carry 1,768,000 million cubic meters out of which only 50% can be put to beneficial uses. In addition, the ground water potential of 422,900 million cubic meters is available for utilisation and about 100,000 million cubic meters is being exploited at present.

The importance given to water in ancient India is reflected in several hymns of the Vedas and epics and narratives from other valuable works such as the *Arthashastra* of Kautilya. Since, India attained independence, water stress has been driven by the growing demands for water from rapidly modernising sectors such as agriculture and industry, not to mention rising domestic demand from expanding urban centres. In the 50 years since 1947, ground water exploitation has been particularly severe in crucial dominant agricultural states like, Punjab, Haryana, Rajasthan and Tamil Nadu. While ground water is being increasingly overexploited in some areas in these states, surface water is being used inadequately or inefficiently. Approximately, 45% of the irrigation water is seeping through unlined field channels. Water-use efficiency in industry is seen to compare unfavourably with countries in the developing as well as the developed world. More significantly, in the 50 years since 1947, per capita water availability has declined from 6000 m^3 to about 2300 m^3.

India's water resources include, 113 river basins, of which 14 rivers are major, 44 are medium and the remaining 55 are minor rivers. The fourteen major river basins account for around 83% of the total area of the basins and contribute 85% of the total surface flow and house 80% of the population served by the basins. The major river basins in India are, the Brahmaputra, the Ganga, Indus, Godavari, Krishna, Mahanadi, Narmada, Cauvery, Brahmani, Tapti, Mahi, Subarnarekha, Pennar, Sabarmati etc.

Rivers

The rivers have nurtured most of the ancient civilisations, which grew along their banks. Even today, from all over the world, millions of people live on the banks of the rivers and are mainly dependent on them for their survival. Rivers are streams of surface water flowing down from a higher altitude to a lower altitude due to the pull of gravity. A river may have its source in a glacier, another in a spring or a lake or a forest. Rivers carry dissolved minerals, organic compounds, small grains of sand, gravel, and other forms of dissolved material as they flow downstream. Rivers originate with small streams, which grow wider as smaller streams and rivers join them along their course across the land. Finally, they drain into seas or oceans. Most rivers with the exception of the River Nile flow towards the Equator. The flow in most rivers is not uniform, which means that sometimes there are floods and sometimes no water flows in them. Flood control projects attempt to reduce the variation in flow.

Today, unfortunately, most of the major rivers of the world are severely polluted, but two of the world's largest river systems-the Amazon that drains a vast area of South America and the Congo in sub-Saharan Africa-remain relatively clean and healthy. This is because both the rivers have few industries and a small human population in their watersheds.

Rivers in India: India has a great number of rivers that are also known for the lifelines of the millions of people living along their banks. These rivers can be classified into four groups: Rivers that flow down from the mighty Himalayas and are supplied by melting snow and glaciers. This is why these are perennial, that is, they never

Rivers in India

dry up during the year. The Deccan Plateau rivers are mainly dependent on rainfall for their water. The coastal rivers, especially those on the west coast are short and do not retain water throughout the year. The rivers in the inland drainage basin of west Rajasthan also depend on the rains. These rivers normally drain towards silt lakes or flow into the sand.

Glaciers

Glaciers are the cover of large sheets of ice that flow down from very high mountains and are often the origin source of snow-feeding rivers. Glaciers are found mainly in places like, Antarctica and Greenland which cover almost 10% of the earth's landmass, varying in size. A glacier is originated to begin life as snowflakes. As occurs more snow falls and gathers the weight of the snow on top compresses the lower layers to form ice. The pile of snow and ice becomes thicker and heavier till a time when the layer of ice at the bottom melts under the pressure. However, it re-freezes almost at once but the process is repeated again and again and as a result, the entire mass begins to slide downhill slowly along the rock surface. A glacier has major impact on the topography of the area, pushing aside boulders, cutting through rocks, and denting its path as it moves.

However, most of the world's glaciers are found at the Poles but they exist in all of the world's continents and even in Africa. Australia does not have any glacier. However, it is considered to be a part of Oceania, which includes several Pacific island chains and the large islands of Papua New Guinea and New Zealand. Both these islands have glaciers. Glaciers require very specific geographical and climatic conditions. Most of them are found in regions of high snowfall in winter and cool temperatures in summer. The amount of rainfall, whether in the form of snowfall, freezing rain, avalanches, or wind-drifted snow, is important for glacier's survival. In the areas like, Siberia and parts of Antarctica, the lack of adequate rainfall prevents glacier development.

Glaciers, In India, are found in the mighty Himalayas. There are about 15,000 glaciers flowing through these mountains which consist of about 17% of the mountain area and feeding many perennial rivers such as the Ganga, Indus, and Brahmaputra. Some of the well-known glaciers are described as under:

Gangotri: This glacier is located in Tehri Garhwal district of Uttaranchal. This is one of the oldest glaciers in the Chaukhamba range where originates the river Ganga. The Gangotri glacier is not a single valley glacier, but a combination of various other glaciers that are fed to it and form a huge mass of ice. This glacier covers an area of 28 km and terminates at Gaumukh (4,000 m).

Pindari: This glacier is one of the most beautiful glaciers in the Kumaon hills. It is also known as the Jewel of Kumaon. It is located at a height of 13,000 feet above sea level between the Nanda Devi and Nandakot peaks and terminates at an altitude of 3,627 metres. Its length is about 5 km long, the snout is about 6 m high and 2.5 m wide and above the snout, the glacier extends for about 3 metre. The Pinder River which originates from the Pindari glacier drains the valley.

Zemu: The Zemu glacier is the largest and most famous glacier in the eastern Himalayas, with a length of about 26 km. It is located in northwestern Sikkim in a U-shaped valley at the base of the Kanchenjunga massif. The Teesta River has its source in this glacier. Many tributary glaciers feed the trunk glacier.

Siachen: Outside the polar world regions, this is the largest glacier in the world, which is stretched over a length of about 72 km. It lies in the extreme north-central part of Jammu and Kashmir near Indo-Tibet border, on the north-facing slopes of the Karakoram Range, and feeds the Shaksgam River that flows into Tibet. The glacier can be accessed from Skardu in Ladakh. To the east of the Siachen, there lies a group of three glaciers which are known as, the Rimo North, Central, and South. Amongst them, these glaciers have almost 700 square km of ice, which, at places, is 100 m deep. Altogether, the glaciers contain about 200 cubic kilometers of ice.

Lakes

A lake is a low-lying part of the Earth's surface in which rainwater, surface water run-off, outflow from a river, and water from other sources accumulates. There is a great variety of lakes on Earth: there

Picture: Lake

are freshwater lakes and saltwater lakes, ranging in size from small fish-ponds to huge water bodies such as Lake Superior in USA which is the world's largest freshwater lake. The Caspian Sea in Europe and the Sambhar lake in Rajasthan are examples of saltwater lakes. India has a large number of lakes spread all over the country, from Kashmir to Kerala and from Rajasthan to Assam. Among the better-known fresh water lakes in India are the Dal lake in Srinagar and the Nainital lake. Whether natural or manmade, all lakes are major sources of water. Lakes are homes to a large variety of aquatic life, with one notable exception: the Dead Sea, a saltwater lake in Israel does not have any form of life. There is too much salt in its water to sustain life.

Around half of the world's lakes are heavily degraded, depleted, and polluted mainly by human activities. The main causes of this pollution are the inflow of domestic sewage, agricultural run-off, discharge of untreated industrial effluents, over-fishing and introduction of exotic species and habitat destruction from population growth, expansion of unplanned cities. As more water is withdrawn for human use which is returned to lakes and rivers is severely polluted and there is less availability of means to maintain vital freshwater ecosystems.

Wetlands

Wetlands, natural and manmade, freshwater or brackish, provide numerous ecological services.

Wetlands provide main habitat to aquatic flora and fauna and various other species of birds, including migratory species. The density of birds and other migratory species is a clear indication of the healthy ecology of a particular wetland. Numerous wetlands, however, have sufficiently unique ecological character as to merit international recognition such as Ramsar Sites.

Wetlands also provide freshwater for agricultural activities, animal husbandry, and for domestic purposes. They also provide drainage services, and livelihoods to fisher-folk. Larger wetlands may also provide an important natural site and resource for sustainable tourism and recreation. They may be considered as an alternative source to power, technology, and capital-intensive municipal sewage plants. However, if used for these purposes without proper reckoning of their assimilative capacity, or for dumping of solid and hazardous waste, they may become severely polluted, leading to adverse impacts on human health.

(Picture: Wetland)

The unintentionally introduction of some alien species of flora in wetlands has also degraded their natural ecological balance. Wetlands are under tremendous pressure from drainage and conversion for farming and human settlements, besides various types of pollution. However, it happens because the public authorities and other individuals having jurisdiction over wetlands area derive some revenues from them, while the alternative use may result in windfall financial gains to them. However, in many instances, the economic values of wetlands environmental services may meaningfully exceed the value from its alternative use. On the other side, due to pollution, the reduction in economic value of their environmental services and the health costs of the pollution itself, are not taken into account while using them as a waste dump. There also does not exist any formal system of wetland rules and regulations outside the international commitments made with respect of Ramsar sites. A holistic approach on wetlands is a vital necessity today which will look at each identified wetland in terms of its causal linkages with other natural entities, human needs, and its own attributes.

Groundwater

Groundwater has been the principle source of drinking water in both urban and rural India. Besides, it is also an important source of water for the agricultural activities and the industrial purposes. Projections for water utilisation by 2000 AD put the groundwater usage at about 50%. Being an important and integral part of the hydrological cycle, groundwater availability depends mainly on the rainfall and recharge conditions. Till recently it had been considered a dependable source of uncontaminated clean water.

However, the demand for groundwater has increased over the years and it has led to water scarcity in many regions of the world. The situation is more aggravated due the problem of water pollution or severe contamination. India is leading towards a freshwater crisis mainly due to faulty management of water resources and environmental degradation. It has led to lack of access to safe water supply to millions of people. The freshwater crisis is already prevalent in many parts of India, varying in scale and intensity depending mainly on the time of the year.

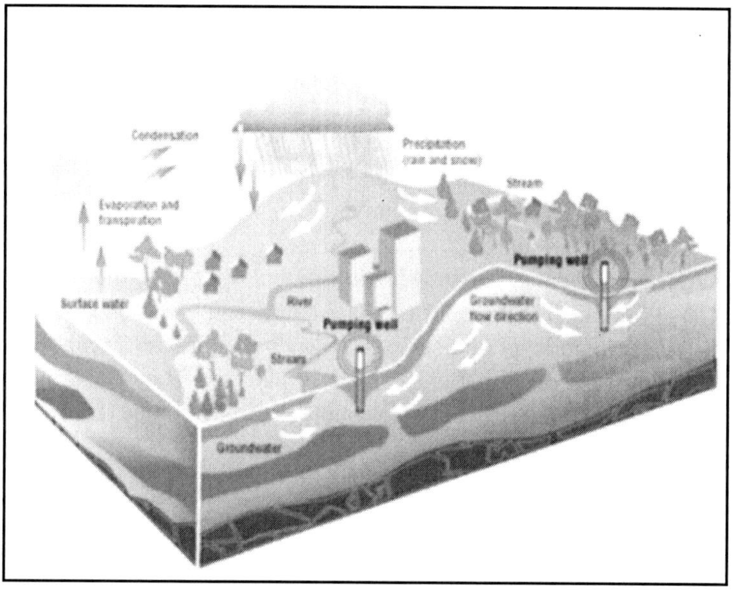

Groundwater

The crisis of groundwater is not a result of natural factors. It has been mainly caused by human activities. During the last two decades, the water level has been rapidly falling in several parts of the country due to an increase in extraction. Numbers of well have been drilled up for irrigation of both food and cash crops which have rapidly and indiscriminately increased. India's fast growing population and changing lifestyles have also increased the domestic use for water. The water requirement for the industry also shows an overall increase. Heavy competition among users like, agriculture, industry, and domestic sectors, is lowering the groundwater table. The groundwater quality is getting highly affected because of the widespread pollution of surface water. Besides, discharge of untreated waste water through bores and leach from unscientific disposal of solid wastes also contaminates groundwater and thus declining the quality of fresh water resources.

However, as far as the quality of groundwater is concerned, several states in the country have been recognised as endemic to 'fluorosis' due to abundance in naturally occurring fluoride-bearing minerals. These states are, Andhra Pradesh, Gujarat, Haryana, Odisha, Punjab, Rajasthan, Tamil Nadu, Uttar Pradesh, Karnataka, Madhya Pradesh, Maharashtra, Bihar, and Delhi. In India, almost half million people suffer from ailments due to excess of fluoride in drinking water. In some districts of Assam and Odisha, groundwater has high iron content. Around 31% of the total area of Rajasthan comes under saline groundwater. Groundwater is saline in almost all of the Bhakra Canal in Punjab and the lift canal system in south-western Haryana. Similarly, high level of arsenic in groundwater has been reported in some districts of West Bengal. Certain places in Haryana, Gujarat, and Andhra Pradesh were also reported to have dangerously high levels of mercury.

Causes of groundwater depletion and contamination

Groundwater is a vital part of the environment, and thus cannot be ignored. There has been a lack of proper attention to groundwater conservation and efficiency in water use, re-use of groundwater recharge, and ecosystem sustainability. An uncontrolled use of the bore well technology has led to the extraction of groundwater at such a high rate that often recharge is not sufficient. The causes of availability of low water in various regions are also directly linked to the declining forest cover and increasing soil degradation.

However, now-a-day, pollution of groundwater resources has become a major problem. The pollution of air, water, and land has an important effect on the pollution and contamination of groundwater. The solid, liquid, and the gaseous waste which are generated through various processes, if not treated properly, results in environmental pollution. This affects groundwater too due to the hydraulic connectivity in the hydrological cycle. Like for example, when air is polluted, rainfall will settle many pollutants on the ground, which can then seep into and contaminate the groundwater resources. Groundwater extraction from the earth without proper recharge and leaching of pollutants from pesticides and fertilisers into the aquifers has polluted groundwater supplies. In addition, leachates from agriculture activities, industrial waste, and the municipal solid waste have also polluted severely surface and ground water. Some 45 million people the world over are affected by water pollution marked by excess fluoride, arsenic, iron, or the ingress of salt water.

What can be done

It is important to realise that groundwater is not a resource that could be utilised unmindfully simply because it is available in abundant quantities. Problems and issues such as water logging, salinity, agricultural toxins, and industrial effluents, all need to be properly looked into.

Other than legislation and checks to conserve and improve the quality of groundwater, society itself plays a very important role. During the last decade there has been a rising awareness among the common people on the need for conservation and development of groundwater. Water use has to be integrated effectively with water regeneration, as was done in many traditional technologies.

However, renovation of forest tanks in drought prone areas will have an important impact on wildlife and forest cover. Similarly, in some urban cities, there need to regenerate groundwater aquifers because of the high degree of dependence on them for drinking water. Rainwater harvesting schemes have been taken up on a wide scale movement in many cities and even made compulsory in some of them.

The temple tanks need to be renovated and urban wetlands are to be protected. These will enhance and bring a rise in the level of groundwater table and a reduction of salt water ingress. Community awareness and freshwater resource management should be encouraged. The government should implement effective groundwater legislation and regulations through self-regulation by local communities and local institutions. External agencies should support the management of freshwater resources. Environmental restoration should be promoted along with household water security.

No single action whether it is community based, legislation, traditional water harvesting systems, or reliance on the market forces will solve the crisis in India. The solution of the freshwater crisis is to integrate conservation and development activities from water extraction to water management at the local level. Also making local communities aware and involving them fully is therefore a key to success. This will ultimately prove the way for combining conservation of the environment with the fulfillment of the basic needs of people.

Water Prevention and Control Act was passed in India by the Parliament in 1974, and by 1990 adopted by all the states. In 1986, the Environment Protection Act was passed by the Indian Parliament. Under both these acts, the states and the central government developed environmental norms and standards for pollution emissions and waste water discharge for different types of sources.

However, groundwater is present in underground aquifers in various parts of the country. Aquifers near the surface are subject to annual recharge from rainfall, but the rate of water recharge is affected by human interference. Deep aquifers, on the other hand, occur below a substratum of hard rock.

The deep aquifers generally contain purest form of water, but since they are recharged only over many millennia, must be protected and conserved for use only in periods of calamitous drought which may happen only once in several hundred years. The boundaries of groundwater aquifers do not generally correspond to the spatial jurisdiction of any local public authorities. Thus, leads to a situation, using groundwater as an open access resource.

The groundwater table has been declining rapidly in various areas of the country in recent decades. This is mainly due to extracting water for agricultural activities, industrial purposes and urban use, in excess of annual recharge. In urban areas also, apart from withdrawals for domestic and industrial use, housing and infrastructure like, roads prevent sufficient recharge of ground water. In addition to this, groundwater pollution also occurs due to leaching and percolating of stored hazardous waste and use of agricultural chemical fertilisers in particular and pesticides. Contamination of groundwater is also due to eugenic causes, such as leaching of arsenic from natural deposits. Since groundwater is the principle source of drinking water, its pollution leads to serious health impacts.

The principle causes of groundwater depletion have their sources in the pricing policies for electricity and diesel. In the case of electricity, where individual metering is not practiced, a normal flat charge for electricity connections makes the marginal cost of electricity to zero. However, subsidies for diesel also reduce the marginal cost of extraction to well below the genuine and efficient level. Given the fact that groundwater is an open access resource for all without the jurisdictions of a particular authority, the user then 'rationally' i.e., in terms of his individual perspective, extracts groundwater until the marginal value to him equals his very low marginal cost of extraction.

However, the results of inefficient extractions of groundwater by all users are leading to the situation of declining of water tables. Support prices for several water intensive agricultural crops with implicit price subsidies aggravate this outcome further by strengthening incentives to take up these crops rather than less water intensive ones.

The declining water tables have several bad social impacts, apart from the likelihood of mining of deep aquifers like, the drinking water source of last resort. The capital costs of pump set and bore wells for groundwater extraction are generally very high when water tables are very deep with no assurance that water would actually be found. In this situation, farmer, who may be a marginal farmer able to borrow the money only at 'usurious rates' of interest, in case water is not found, finds it very difficult to repay his debts. This may lead to his destitution or even more worst conditions. However, if the impacts were not so dire, there would be excessive use of electricity and diesel.

Thus, the efficient use of groundwater is required the practice of non-metering of electric supply to farmers be discontinued in their own enlightened self-interest. It would be necessary to progressively ensure that the environmental impacts are taken into proper account in setting electricity tariffs, and diesel pricing. Increased run-off of rainfall water in urban areas due to impermeable structures and infrastructure prevents groundwater recharge. This is an additional cause of falling water tables in urban areas. In rural areas several cost-effective contour bonding techniques have been proved to be effective in enhancing groundwater recharge. A number of effective traditional water management techniques to recharge groundwater have been stopped by the local communities due to the onset of pump sets extraction, and need to be revived. Finally, increase in tree cover, is also effective in improving groundwater recharge.

Water, Soil, Air and Noise Pollution: Their Causes and Consequences

Pollution can be understood as an effect of undesirable changes in our natural environment that has adverse impacts on plants, animals and human beings. This occurs when only short-term economic interests are fulfilled at the cost of long-term ecological benefits for humanity. Pollutant materials include solid, liquid or gaseous substances present in greater than natural abundance, produced due to human activities, which have a detrimental effect on our environment.

WATER POLLUTION

> "Our liquid planet glows like a soft blue sapphire in the hard-edged darkness of space. There is nothing else like it in the solar system. It is because of water."
>
> **-John Todd.**

Water is one of the prime necessities of life. Without water there would be no life. We usually take water for granted. It flows from our taps when they are turned on; most of us are able to bathe when we want to, swim when we choose and water our gardens. Like good health we ignore water when we have it. Although 71% of the Earth's surface is covered by water, only a tiny fraction of this water is available to us as freshwater. About 97% of the total water available on Earth is found in the oceans and is too salty for drinking or irrigation. The remaining 3% is fresh water. Of this, 2.997% is locked in ice caps or glaciers. Thus, only 0.003% of the Earth's total volume of water is easily available to us as soil moisture, groundwater, water vapour and the water in lakes, streams, rivers and wetlands. In short, if the world's water supply were only 100 liters our usable supply of freshwater would be only about 0.003 liters (one-half teaspoon).

This makes water a very important and useful natural resource. We cannot ignore the importance of water and cannot deny that the future wars in our world may well be fought over water. By the middle of this century, almost twice as many people will be trying to share the same amount of freshwater which the Earth has now. In the future, as freshwater becomes a scarce resource, the access to water will be an important factor in determining the economic growth of many countries around the world. The water that is found in streams, rivers, lakes, wetlands and artificial reservoirs is called surface water. Water that percolates and leaches into the ground and fills the pores in soil and rock is called groundwater. Porous water-saturated layers of sand, gravel or bedrock through which ground water flows are called *aquifers*. Most aquifers are replenished naturally by rainfall that percolates downward through the soil and rock. This process is called natural recharge.

If the withdrawal rate of an aquifer exceeds through its natural recharge rate, the water table is lowered. Any pollutant that is discharged onto the land above is also pulled into the aquifer and pollutes the groundwater, resulting in polluted water in the nearby wells.

India receives most of her precipitation from the south-west monsoon during the months of June to September due to the seasonal winds and the differences in temperature between the land and the sea. These seasonal winds blow from the subcontinent to oceans during the winter. The Indian monsoon is usually reasonably stable but varies geographically. In some years, the beginning of the rains may be delayed considerably over the entire country or a part of it. The rains may also end earlier than usual. The rainfall may be heavier over one part than another. All these can cause local floods or drought. In India, however, even such areas which receive adequate rainfall during the monsoon season suffer from shortages in the post-monsoon period due to the lack of proper storage facilities.

When the composition of water quality changes directly or indirectly resulting from man's activities such that water becomes unfit for any purpose, it is said to be polluted.

With the increasing number of human population's dependence on water resources, it has become a scarce commodity. Pollution makes even the limited available water unfit for human use. Water is considered to be polluted when there is any physical, biological or chemical change in the quality of water that adversely affects living organisms or makes water unsuitable for their use.

In other words, water pollution is the introduction of chemical, physical or biological materials into fresh or ocean waters that reduces the quality of the water and affects the living organisms in it. This process ranges from simple addition of dissolved or suspended solid materials to discharge of the most insidious and persistent toxic pollutant materials like, pesticides, heavy metals, and non-degradable, bio-accumulative, chemical compounds. Similarly, in other words, it could be said that water pollution is caused by the industrial waste products drained into lakes, rivers, and other water bodies. It has made marine life no longer hospitable and suitable for further use. Humans pollute water with large scale disposal of garbage, sewage, flowers, ashes and another household waste etc. In rural areas also, one can find people bathing and cooking in the same water, making it incredibly filthy.

Picture: Water Pollution

However, there are various classes of common water pollutant materials. These are disease-causing agents like, pathogens, which include bacteria, viruses, protozoa and parasitic worms that enter water from domestic sewage and untreated human and animal wastes. Human wastes consist of concentrated populations of coliform bacteria such as *Escherichia coli* and *Streptococcus faecalis*. These bacteria normally grow in large intestine of the human body and are responsible for some food digestion and also for the production of vitamin K. These bacteria are not harmful in low numbers but large numbers of these bacteria cause gastrointestinal diseases. Other potentially harmful bacteria in smaller number may also be present in human wastes. Thus, greater the amount of waste in water, the greater is the chance of contracting disease from them.

Acid rain further adds to the pollution in water. In addition to these, thermal pollution and the depletion of dissolved oxygen aggravate the already worsened condition of the water bodies. The amount of oxygen required to break down a certain amount of organic matter is called the biological oxygen demand (BOD). Water pollution can also indirectly occur as an offshoot of soil pollution – through surface runoff and leaching to groundwater.

Conventional

Classical or conventional pollutants are normally associated with the direct input of human waste products. With the growing of urbanisation and rapid increase in human population has created severe sewage problems because treatment facilities have not kept pace with need. However, untreated and partially treated sewage from municipal wastewater systems and septic tanks in un-severed areas contribute large quantities of nutrients and suspended solids, dissolved solids, oil, metals like, arsenic, mercury, chromium, lead, iron, and manganese, and biodegradable organic carbon to the water environment.

These conventional pollutants may cause a numerous water pollution problem. Excess release of suspended solids, block out energy from the Sun and thus affect the carbon dioxide-oxygen conversion process, which is the vital to process to maintain the biological food chain. Also, large concentrations of suspended solids wastes silt up rivers and navigational channels, necessitating frequent dredging. Excess dissolved solids make the water undesirable for drinking and for agricultural irrigation.

It is also essential to the aquatic habitat, nutrients such as nitrogen and phosphorus may also cause over fertilisation and accelerate the natural aging process i.e., eutrophication of lakes. This increase in turn produces an overgrowth of aquatic vegetation and massive algal blooms, and an overall shift in the biologic community from low productivity with various diverse species to high productivity with great numbers of a few species of a less desirable nature. Bacterial action oxidizes biodegradable organic carbon and consumes dissolved oxygen in the water. In the extreme cases where the organic-carbon loading is high the oxygen consumption may lead to an oxygen depression like, less than 2 mg/l compared with 5 to 7 mg/l for a healthy stream, which is sufficient to cause a fish kill and seriously disturb the growth of associated organisms that require oxygen to survive.

Nonconventional

The nonconventional pollutants consist of dissolved and particulate forms of both toxic metals and nontoxic metals, and degradable and persistent organic carbon compounds discharged into water as a by-product of industrial sectors or as an integral part of marketable products. Annually, more than 13,000 incidents of oil spills of varying magnitude occur in the United States. Thousands of environmentally untested chemicals are frequently discharged into waterways, and an estimated of over 400 to 500 new compounds are marketed each year. In addition to this, coal strip mining releases chemical acid wastes that spoil the surrounding waterways. Nonconventional pollutants may vary from biologically inert materials such as clay and iron residues to the most toxic and insidious materials such as halogenated hydrocarbons like, DDT, ketone, mirex, and polychlorinated biphenyls. The latter group may cause damage ranging from acute biological effects like, complete sterilisation of stretches of waterways to chronic sub-lethal effects that may go undetected for years. The chronic low-level pollutants are proving to be the most difficult to treat and abate because of their ubiquitous nature and long chemical stability.

Sources of the pollution of water are mainly because of factories, power plants, coal mines and oil wells situated either close to water source or away from sources. They discharge pollutants directly or indirectly into the water sources like river, lakes, water streams etc. The harmful effects of water pollution are as follows:

(a) Human beings become victims of numerous water borne diseases like, typhoid, cholera, dysentery, hepatitis, jaundice, etc.

(b) The presence of acids or alkali in water destroys the life of microorganisms, thereby hindering the self-purification process of water bodies or rivers. Agricultural activities are affected severely due to polluted water. Marine eco-systems are affected adversely.

(c) The urban sewage waste propagates growth of phytoplankton in water bodies; causing reduction of dissolved oxygen.

(d) Poisonous nature of industrial wastes presents in water bodies badly affect the fish population and deprives us of one of our sources of food. It also kills other living animals in fresh water.

(e) The underground water quality is also affected due to the presence of toxicity and pollutant content of surface water.

Water pollution by industries and its effects - A change in the chemical, physical, biological, and radiological quality of water that is injurious to its uses. The term "water pollution" generally refers to human-induced changes to water quality. Thus, the discharge of toxic chemicals from industries or the release of human or livestock waste into a nearby water body is considered pollution.

However, the contamination of groundwater of water bodies such as rivers, lakes, wetlands, estuaries, and oceans can threaten the health of humans and aquatic life. Sources of water pollution can be divided into two categories (i) Point-source pollution where contaminants are discharged from a discrete location. For example, sewage outfalls and oil spills are examples of point-source pollution (ii) Non-point-source, where all the other discharges that delivers contaminants to water bodies. For example, acid rain and unconfined runoff from agricultural or urban areas falls under this category.

The major contaminants of water include heavy toxic chemicals, nutrients, biodegradable organics, and bacterial and viral pathogens. Water pollution can severely affect human health when pollutants enter the body either through skin exposure or through the direct consumption of contaminated drinking water and contaminated food. Prime pollutants, consist DDT and polychlorinated biphenyls which persist in the natural environment and bioaccumulation occurs in the tissues of aquatic organisms. These prolonged and persistent organic pollutants are transferred to the food chain and they can reach levels of concern in fish species that are eaten by human beings. Moreover, bacterial and viral pathogens can pose a public health risk for those who drink contaminated water or eat raw shellfish from polluted water bodies.

However, water contaminants have a significant impact on aquatic ecosystems. Water bodies with the enrichments of nutrients like, nitrogen and phosphorus, may result in the growth of algae and other aquatic plants that clog streams. However, if wastewater contains biodegradable organic matter and is discharged into a stream with inadequate dissolved oxygen, the point of downstream water discharge will become anaerobic and thus will be muddy and dark. Settleable solids will be silted on the streambed, and anaerobic decomposition will occur. Over the reach of stream where the concentration of dissolved-oxygen is zero, a zone of putrefaction will occur with the production of hydrogen sulfide, ammonia and other odorous gases. Fish species require a minimum of 4-5 mg of dissolved oxygen per liter of water and in the absence of dissolve oxygen they will be unable to survive in the stream.

However, direct exposures to toxic chemicals are also dangerous for the health of individual aquatic plants and animals. Chemicals like, pesticides are frequently transported to lakes and rivers through runoff water and they can have severe effects on aquatic life. Toxic chemicals have been proved to reduce the growth, survival, reproductive output, and disease resistance of the concerned exposed organisms. These effects can have significant consequences for the viability of aquatic populations and communities.

CASE STUDY

The worst oil spill disasters have occurred in the *Exxon Valdez*. On 24th March 1989, the Exxon Valdez, a tanker more than three football fields wide, went off course in a 16 km-wide channel in Prince William Sound near Valdez in Alaska. It hit submerged rocks, creating an environmental disaster. The rapidly spreading oil slick coated more than 1600 km of shoreline killing between 300,000-645,000 water birds and large number of sea otters, harbor seals, whales and fish. Exxon spent 2.2 billion dollars directly on the clean-up operations. However, some results of the clean-up effort showed that where high-pressure jets of hot water were used to clean beaches, coastal plants and animals that had survived the spill were killed. Thus, it did more harm than good. Exxon pleaded guilty in 1991 and agreed to pay the Federal Government and the state of Alaska 1 billion in fines and civil damages. This 8.5-billion-dollar accident might have been

Picture: Pumping up of Ground Water

prevented if Exxon had spent only 22.5 million dollars to fit the tanker with a double hull-one inside the other. Such double-hulled vessels would be less likely to rupture and spill their contents. The spill highlighted the urgent need for the protection of marine ecosystem.

Groundwater Pollution: where oil spills attract attention of mass media at large, there is much severe threat to human life which comes from our groundwater, which is used for drinking water and crops irrigation, being highly polluted. While groundwater is easy to exploit and deplete and thus pollute, it gets renewed at very slow rate and hence must be used judiciously. Groundwater flows are slow and not turbulent.

Thus, the contaminants are not effectively diluted and easily dispersed as by surface water. Moreover, the pumping groundwater and treating it, is very slow and costly. So it is extremely necessary to prevent the groundwater pollution in the first place. Some major causes of groundwater pollution are:

- Urban run-off untreated water or poorly treated waste water and garbage.
- Industrial waste storage located above or near aquifers.
- Agricultural practices in rural areas such as application of large amounts of chemical fertilisers and pesticides, animal feeding operations, etc.
- Leaks from underground storage tanks containing gasoline and other hazardous substances.
- Leached from landfills.
- Poorly-designed and inadequately maintained septic tanks.
- Mining wastes.

Several cases of arsenic poisoning from contaminated groundwater have been reported from West Bengal in what we known today as the worst case of groundwater pollution. The groundwater arsenic contamination in West Bengal was first reported in local daily newspaper in December 1983, when 63 people from three villages located in different districts were identified by health officials as suffering from arsenic poisoning. Arsenic poisoning brings with its other complications like liver and spleen enlargement, cirrhosis of the liver, diabetes, goiter and skin cancers.

Wastewater discharges are most commonly controlled through effluent standards and discharge permits. Under this system, discharge permits are issued with limits on the quantity and quality of effluents. Water-quality standards are sets of qualitative and quantitative criteria designed to improve the quality of receiving waters. However, criteria can be developed and implemented to preserve and protect aquatic life against severe and chronic effects and to safeguard humans against harmful health effects, including cancer.

LAND-POLLUTION

We neither can manufacture soil with a tank of chemical materials nor can we invent a rainforest or produce a single bird. We can only enhance the fertility of soil by helping its processes along, but we can never recreate what we destroy. The soil is a natural resource for which there is no alternative. The soil is a thin covering over the land comprising of a mixture of minerals, organic material, living organisms, air and water, that together support the growth of plant life. Various factors contribute to the formation of soil from the parent rock material. This includes the mechanical weathering of rocks due to changes in temperature and abrasion, wind, moving water, glaciers, chemical weathering activities and lichens. Climate and time are also an important factor in the development of the soils. In dry or cold climate, soils develop very slowly, while in warm and humid climates soils develop more rapidly. Under ideal climatic conditions, soft parent material may develop into 1 cm of soil in 15 years. Under poor climatic conditions, a hard parent rock material may require hundreds of years to develop into mature soil.

Mature soils are arranged in a layer of series of zones called 'soil horizons'. Each horizon has a distinct texture and composition that varies with different types of soils. A cross-sectional view of the horizons in a soil is called a 'Soil profile'.

The top layer of soil surface is called the 'O-horizon' which consists mostly of freshly-fallen and partially-decomposed leaves, twigs, animal waste, fungi and other organic materials. Normally, it is brown or black.

The uppermost layer of the soil is called the 'A-horizon' which consists of partially-decomposed organic matter like, humus and some inorganic mineral particles. It is usually dark black and looser than the deeper layers. The roots of most of the plants are found in these two upper layers. As long as these soil layers are anchored by vegetation, the soil stores water and releases it in a trickle throughout the year instead of a force like a flood. These two top layers also contain a large number of bacteria, fungi, nutrients, and contribute to soil fertility.

The 'B-horizon', is called the subsoil which contains less organic material and fewer organisms than the A-horizon. The area of the horizon below the subsoil is called the 'C-horizon' and that are consists of weathered parent material. However, this parent material does not consist of any organic material. The chemical composition of the C-horizon layer helps to determine the pH of the soil and also influences the soil's rate of water absorption and retention.

Soils vary in their content of clay (very fine particles), silt (fine particles), sand (medium size particle), and gravel (coarse to very coarse particles). The relative amounts of the different sizes and types of mineral particles determine the soil texture. Soil with approximately equal mixtures of clay, sand and humus are called loams.

Land pollution is the degradation of the Earth's land surface through misuse of the soil by poor agricultural practices, mineral exploitation, industrial waste dumping, and indiscriminate disposal of urban wastes. Soil is a complex mixture of living and non-living materials. It provides anchorage and sustenance to plants. Natural agents like water and wind, constantly tend to remove the top soil and cause erosion. The falling of the rain upon the unprotected top soils washes it down into the streams. In the absence of plant cover the eroded soils cannot hold water. Waster rushes into the rivers and overflows as flood streams. Dust storm also causes soil erosion. The materials of the top soil are picked up in such quantities that they form dust clouds. Human beings also cause soil erosion.

Picture: Land Pollution

The increasing human habitation and expansion of unplanned urban areas lead to removal of vegetation cover. Once vegetation is cleared, the naked soils get exposed to wind and water. Improper tillage is another factor of soil erosion. Farmers are however loose the top soil for removing weeds and preparing seed beds. They also leave agricultural fields lying fallow for long time. These practices expose the top soil to the wind and hence, cause erosion.

Soil erosion is a result of the unwise use of human's actions like, overgrazing or faulty practices of cultivation. These leave the land unprotected and vulnerable to soil erosion. However, accelerated soil erosion by water or wind may affect both agricultural areas and the natural environment. It is also one of the most widespread issues of today's environmental problems. Soil erosion is just one form of soil degradation. Other kinds of soil degradation include Salinisation, vital nutrient loss, and compaction.

Soil-Misuse

Soil erosion is a result of faulty agricultural practices which removes rich humus topsoil developed over years through the decay of vegetative and microbial degradation and thus strips the land of valuable nutrients for the growth of crops. Strip mining for coal and minerals lays waste thousands of acres of land annually. Denuding the Earth and subjecting the area of mines are widespread problems of soil erosion. The rapid increase in urbanisation due to heavy population pressure presents additional soil-erosion problems. However, sediment loads in nearby streams may increase as much as 500 to 1,000 times over to that was recorded in nearby undeveloped stretches of stream. Thus, soil erosion not only despoils the quality of the Earth for farming and other uses, but also increases the suspended-solids load of the waterway. This increase interferes with the ecological habitat and poses silting problems in navigation channels, inhibiting its commercial use of these waters.

Picture: Soil Erosion

Prevention of soil erosion -Plant provides protective cover on the soil and prevents its erosion for the reasons:

(a) Plants slow down the speed of running water as it flows over the land and this allows much of the rain to soak into the ground;

(b) Roots of plant hold the soil and prevent it from being washed away;

(c) Plants break the impact of a raindrop before it hits the soil, thus reducing its ability to erode;

(d) Vegetations in wetlands and on the banks of rivers are of importance as they slow down the flow of the water and their roots bind the soil, thus preventing soil erosion.

Preventing soil erosion requires technical changes to adopt. Aspects of technical changes include:

(i) Use of contour ploughing and wind breaks;

(ii) Leaving unploughed grass strips between ploughed lands;

(iii) Make sure that there are plants growing on the soil, and that the soil is rich in humus like, decaying plant and animal remains. This organic matter is the 'glue' that binds the soil particles together and plays a significant role in preventing soil erosion;

(iv) Avoid overgrazing and the over-use of crop lands;

(v) Allowing the indigenous plants to grow along the banks of river instead of ploughing and planting crops right up to the water's edge;

(vi) Promoting biological diversity by planting several different types of plants together;

(vii) Conservation of wetlands;

(viii) Organic agriculture;

(ix) Crop rotation.

We can check the erosion of soil by adopting the following additional practices:

1. Practice of intensive cropping and use of proper drainage canals.
2. Terracing on the sloping fields. This retards the speed of the flowing water.
3. Planting trees and sowing grasses.
4. Extensive afforestation practices to be carried out.

AIR POLLUTION

The history of the origin of air pollution on this earth can be dated back to the times when man for the first time started using firewood as a means of cooking and heating. Hippocrates also has mentioned air pollution in 400 BC. However, with the discovery and increased use of fossil fuel like, coal, air pollution became more pronounced especially in the urban areas. However, as a problem, it was recognised 700 years ago in London in the form of smoke pollution, which prompted King Edward I to formulate the first anti-pollution law to restrict people from using coal for domestic heating in the year 1273. Later, in the year 1300 AD, another Act was passed banning the use of coal; defying the law led to imposition of capital punishment. In spite of this law, air pollution became a serious problem in London due to widespread use of coal during the Industrial Revolution. The earliest recorded major disaster was the 'London Smog' which occurred in 1952 AD, which resulted in more than 4000 deaths due to the concentration of air pollutants over the city for five days.

In the middle of the 19th century in Europe, a black form of the Peppered moth began appearing in industrial areas. Generally, a normal-coloured Peppered moth is well camouflaged when on a clean, lichen-covered tree. However, this moth was easily spotted and picked up by birds on the smoke-blackened bark of trees in industrial areas. So, while the normal pepper-patterned moths were successful in surviving in clean non-industrial areas, only black-coloured moths were successfully camouflaged in industrial areas. Thus, with the rapid increase of industrialisation, an increased incidence of black forms was observed not only in the peppered moth, but also many other moths. This is a unique and classic case of pollution leading to adaptation.

Air pollution started increasing in the beginning of the 20th century with the advancement in transportation system and large-scale use of diesel and petrol. The severe problem of air quality was due to the formation of petrochemical smog from the combustion residues of diesel and petrol engines which were felt for the first time in Los

Angeles. Pollution due to auto-exhaust remains a serious environmental issue in many developed and developing countries, including India.

Air Pollution

Air Pollution Control Act was passed 1981 in India and the Motor Vehicle Act for controlling air pollution was passed very recently. These laws are mainly intended to prevent the air from being severely polluted.

One of the greatest industrial disasters leading to serious air pollution took place in Bhopal district of Madhya Pradesh on December 2nd, 1984, where the extremely poisonous methyl isocyanate gas was accidentally released from the Union Carbide's pesticide manufacturing plant. The effects of this disaster on human health and the soil are felt even today.

Air pollution is the concentration and accumulation of harmful gases in the atmosphere that, endanger human health or produce other measured effects on living matter and other materials. Among the principle sources of pollution are power and heat generation, the burning of solid wastes, industrial processes, and, especially, transportation.

Air pollution is by far the most harmful form of pollution in our environment. Air pollution is caused by the injurious smoke emitted by cars, buses, trucks, trains, and factories, namely Sulphur dioxide, carbon monoxide and nitrogen oxides, hydrocarbons, particulates, photochemical oxidants. Chlorofluorocarbons (CFC), released from refrigerators, air-conditioners, deodorants and insect repellents cause severe damage to the Earth's environment. This gas has slowly damaged the atmosphere and depleted the ozone layer leading to global warming.

Even smoke of the burning leaves and bidi and cigarettes are harmful to the natural environment causing a major damage to man and the atmosphere. However, the evidences of increasing air pollution are seen in the disease like, lung cancer, asthma, allergies, and various breathing problems along with severe and irreparable damage to flora and fauna. However, most natural phenomenon of migratory birds has been badly affected with severe air pollution preventing them from reaching their seasonal metropolitan destinations of centuries.

Air is mainly a mixture of various gases such as oxygen, carbon dioxide, nitrogen. These are present in a particular ratio. Whenever there is any imbalance in the ratio of these gases, air pollution is caused. The sources of air pollution can be grouped as under:

(i) Natural- like forest fires, ash from smoking volcanoes, dust storm and decay of organic matters.

(ii) Man-made- due to over population, deforestation, urbanisation and industrialisation.

Certain human activities release numerous pollutants in air like, carbon monoxide, sulfur dioxide, hydrocarbons, oxides of nitrogen, lead, arsenic, asbestos, radioactive matter, and dust. However, the major threats come from burning of the fossil fuels like, coal and petroleum products. Thermal power plants, automobiles and industries are major sources of air pollution as well. Due to significant progress in atomic energy sector, there has been an increase in the concentration of radioactivity in the atmosphere. Mining activities add to air pollution in the form of particulate matter. Progress in agriculture practices due to use of chemical fertilisers and pesticides has also contributed towards air pollution. Indiscriminate and frequent cutting of trees and clearing of forestland has led to increase in the amount of carbon dioxide in atmosphere. Global warming is a consequence of greenhouse effect caused by increased level of carbon dioxide (CO^2). Ozone (O^3) depletion has resulted in UV radiation striking our earth.

The gaseous composition of unpolluted air

The Gases	*Parts per million (vol.)*
Nitrogen	756,500
Oxygen	202,900
Water	31,200
Argon	9,000
Carbon Dioxide	305
Neon	17.4
Helium	5.0
Methane	0.97-1.16
Krypton	0.97
Nitrous oxide	0.49
Hydrogen	0.49
Xenon	0.08
Organic vapours	ca.0.02

Harmful Effects of air pollution –

(a) Air pollution affects respiratory system of living organisms and causes bronchitis, asthma, lung cancer, pneumonia etc. Carbon monoxide emitted from motor vehicles and cigarette smoke affects the central nervous system.

(b) Due to depletion of ozone layer, UV radiation reaches the earth. UV radiation causes skin cancer, damage to eyes and immune system.

Ozone is formed of oxygen with three atoms. It is produced naturally from the process of photo dissociation of oxygen gas molecules in the atmosphere. The ozone, thus formed, is however, broken down constantly by naturally-occurring processes which maintain its balance in the ozone layer. In the absence of pollutant materials, the creation and breakdown of ozone gas are purely governed by natural forces, but the presence of certain pollutants can increase the breakdown of ozone. It was known earlier that ozone shows fluctuations in its concentrations, sometimes accompanied by a little ozone depletion. However, in 1985 the large-scale destruction of the ozone also called 'Ozone Hole' came into light, when some British researchers published measurements about the ozone layer.

Soon after these findings much emphasis was given to research on ozone layer, which convincingly established that CFCs were leading to its depletion. These CFCs (chlorofluorocarbons) are extremely stable, non-flammable, non-toxic and easy to handle. This makes them ideal for many industrial uses such as aerosols, air-conditioners, refrigerators and fire extinguishers. Many cans, which give out foams and sprays, use CFC (e.g., perfumes, room-fresheners etc.). Chlorofluorocarbons are also used in making foam for mattresses and cushions, disposable Styrofoam cups, glasses, packaging material for insulation, cold storage, etc. However, their stability also gives them a long life-span in the atmosphere.

Halons are also similar in structure to the CFCs but contain bromine atoms instead of chlorine. They are more dangerous to the ozone layer than CFCs. Halons are also used as fire-extinguishing agents as they do not harm the people and equipment exposed to them during firefighting.

The CFCs and halons are migrated into the upper atmosphere after they are released. As they are heavier than air, they have to be carried by air current up to a point just above the lower atmosphere and then they slowly spread into the upper atmosphere. This is a very slow process and may take as long as five to fifteen years.

It is a fact that CFCs are evenly distributed over the globe but the depletion of ozone is especially pronounced over the south-pole, due to the extreme weather conditions in the Antarctica atmosphere. The ozone layer over countries like Australia, New Zealand, South Africa and parts of South America is also depleted. India has signed the Montreal Protocol in 1992, which is aimed at controlling the production and consumption of ozone-depleting substances.

(c) **Acid rain** is a result of air pollution. Acid rain, or acid deposition, is a broad term that includes any form of precipitation with acidic components, such as sulfuric or nitric acid that fall to the ground from the atmosphere in wet or dry forms. This can include rain, snow, fog, hail or even dust that is acidic. It is caused by the presence of nitrogen oxides and sulfur dioxide in the air. These oxides dissolve in rain water to form nitric acid and sulfuric acid respectively. Various monuments, buildings, and statues are damaged due to corrosion by acid present in the rain. Due to acid rain soil also becomes acidic. The cumulative effect is the gradual degradation of soil and a decline in forest and agricultural productivity.

(d) The greenhouse gases like, carbon dioxide (CO^2) and methane (CH^4) trap the heat radiated from earth. This leads to an increase in earth's temperature.

(e) Some harmful toxic metals and pesticides also cause air pollution.

Local-and-Regional

Smog has seriously affected more persons than any other type of air pollution. It can be loosely defined as a multisource, widespread air pollution that occurs in the air of cities. Smog, a contraction of the words smokes and fog, has been caused throughout recorded history by water condensing on smoke particles, usually from burning coal. The infamous London fogs of 1952 about 4,000 deaths were attributed to the severe smog of this type. Another type, ice fog, occurs only at high latitudes and extremely low temperatures and is a combination of smoke particles and ice crystals.

However, as the coal economy gradually replaced by a petroleum economy, photochemical smog became predominant in many cities. Its unpleasant properties resulted from the irradiation by sunlight of hydrocarbons are primarily the unburnt gasoline emitted by automobiles and other combustion sources, and other pollutants in the air. Irradiation produces a long series of photochemical reactions.

The products of the reactions consist of organic particles, ozone, aldehydes, ketones, peroxyacetyl nitrate, and organic acids and other oxidants. Sulfur dioxide, which is always present to some extent, oxidizes and hydrates to form sulfuric acid and become part of the particulate matter. Furthermore, automobiles are polluters even in the absence of photochemical reactions. They are mostly responsible for much of the particulate material in the air. They also emit carbon monoxide as one of the most toxic constituents of smog.

However, all types of smog reduce visibility and, with an exception of ice fog, are irritating to the respiratory system. Statistical studies, however, show that smog is a contributor to malignancies of many types. Photochemical smog produces eye irritation and lacrimation and causes severe damage to many types of natural vegetation, including crops. Acute effects include an increased mortality rate, especially among persons suffering from respiratory and coronary ailments. Air pollution also has a deleterious effect on works of art.

Air pollution on a regional scale is the result of local air pollution which includes individual sources like, automobiles-that has spread out to cover areas of thousands of square kilometers. Concentrations of air-pollution at any given place, especially locally and regionally are influenced by meteorological conditions and landforms. For example, cities located in bowls or valleys over which atmospheric inversions form and act as imperfect lids are likely to suffer from incidences of severe smog. Oxides of sulfur and nitrogen are carried long distances by the atmosphere and then precipitated in the form of solution as acid rain which causes serious damage to vegetation, waterways, and buildings.

Global

Human beings pollute the atmosphere severely on a global scale. Till the early 1970s little attention was paid to the possible harmful effects like, pollution. Measurements in the Hawaii islands suggest that carbon dioxide concentration in the atmosphere is increasing at a rate of about 0.2% every year. The effect of this rapid increase may alter the climate of the Earth by increasing the average global temperature. However, certain pollutants decrease the concentration of ozone occurring naturally in the stratosphere, which in turn increases the volume of ultraviolet radiation reaching the Earth's surface. Such radiation may damage natural vegetation and increase the skin cancer problem. Examples of stratospheric contaminants include nitrogen oxides emitted by supersonic aircraft and chlorofluorocarbons used in refrigerators and aerosol which can act as propellants. The chlorofluorocarbons reach the stratosphere by upward mixing from the lower parts of the atmosphere. However, it is believed that these chemicals are responsible for the significant loss of ozone layer over the Polar Regions.

C. Fundamentals of prevention and control of air pollution

Air pollutants can be described as gaseous or particulate matters. Different techniques for controlling these pollutants are discussed below:

(a) Methods of controlling gaseous pollutants-

1. *Combustion-* is used for organic and vapour form of the pollutants. During flame combustion or catalytic process, these organic pollutants are converted into water vapour and relatively less harmful products like, CO^2.
2. *Absorption-* In this technique, the gaseous effluents are passed through scrubbers or absorbers. These contain a suitable liquid absorbent, which removes or modifies one or more of the pollutants present in the gaseous effluents.
3. *Adsorption-* In this method, the gaseous effluents are passed through porous solid adsorbents which are kept in suitable containers. The organic and inorganic constituents of the effluent gases are trapped at the interface of the solid adsorbent by physical adsorbent.

(b) Methods to control particulate emissions-

1. The mechanical device generally works as:
   (i) *Gravity:* The particles are settled down by gravitational force.

(ii) Sudden change in the direction of flow of gas. This causes the particles to separate out due to greater momentum.

2. *Fabric Filters:* The gases containing dust are passed through a porous medium. These porous media may be woven or filled fabrics. The particles present in the gas are trapped and collected in the filters. The gases freed from the particles are discharged.
3. *Wet Scrubbers:* are used in chemical, mining and metallurgical industries to trap SO_2, NH_3, metal fumes, etc.
4. *Electrostatic Precipitators:* are used when a gas or an air stream containing aerosols in the form of dust, fumes or mist, is passed between two electrodes, then, the aerosol particles get precipitated on the electrode.

(c) Other practices in controlling air pollution - Apart from the above, following practices also help in controlling air pollution:

(i) Use of proper designed equipment's and smokeless fuels, hearths in industries and at home.

(ii) Automobiles should be properly maintained and adhere to recent emission-control standards.

(iii) Trees are to be planted along road side and houses.

(iv) Alternative energy sources like, wind, solar energy, ocean currents, should fulfill energy needs.

(v) Tall chimneys should be installed for vertical dispersion of pollutants.

(d) General air pollution control devices/equipment's for industries- The frequently used equipment's or process for control of dust in various industries are: (a) Mechanical dust collectors in the form of dust cyclones; (b) Electrostatic precipitators- both for dry and wet system; (c) Particulate scrubbers; (d) Spray of water at dust generation points; (e) Good ventilation system and (f) significant numbers of monitoring devices to know the concentration of dust in general body of air.

The common equipment's are used for control of toxic or flue gases are the: (a) desulphurisation process; (b) denitrification process; (c) gas conditioning and (d) Various monitoring devices to know the efficacy of the systems used.

(e) Steps are to be taken for the reduction of air pollution- Change of human behaviour in order to reduce air pollution at home as well as on road. However, the following steps can be taken by all of us to clean our Environment.

At Home:

1. Avoid using chemical pesticides or chemical fertilisers in your yard and garden. Various types of fertilisers are a source of nitrous oxide, a greenhouse gas that contributes to global warming. Use organic products instead.
2. Do not burn but compost your yard waste. Outdoor burning pollutes atmospheric air. Breathing this smoke is bad for you, your family and your neighbours. Also, you can use the compost in your garden.
3. If you are using a wood stove or fireplace to heat your home, it would be better to switch another form of heat as it does not produce smoke. It is always better to use sweater or warm clothing than using fireplace.
4. Be energy efficient- to keep your atmosphere free from air pollution. Keep your home well-maintained with weather-stripping, properly ventilated and insulated. Lowering your thermostat can also help to save two percent on your heating bill.
5. Forestation and encourage others to plant trees as well. Tree absorbs and stores carbon dioxide from the atmosphere, and filters out the air pollution. During warmer days, trees provide cool air and avoid unnecessary use of energy on air conditioning.
6. Stop smoking at home, at office or at outside at public places. Tobacco smoking not only deteriorates self's health, it affects others' health too.

On the Road:

7. Keep your vehicle well maintained. It reduces fuel consumption. However, a poorly maintained engine both creates more air pollution and uses more fuel. Replace oil and air filters regularly, and keep your tires properly inflated.
8. Drive less. Walking, bicycling, travelling in the bus, or working from home can save you money as well as reduce air pollution.
9. Switch off your engine at traffic signals. If you stop for more than 30 seconds, except in traffic, turn off your engine.
10. Use public buses and if possible keep only one vehicle and not more than that. The more vehicles you use, more fuels are used and the more air pollution it causes.

NOISE POLLUTION

Noise pollution has been a problem of relatively recent origin. Noise pollution is a composite of sounds generated by human activities ranging from vehicles horn, blasting stereo systems to the roar of ballistic missile and supersonic transport jets. However, the frequency of noise may be of significant importance as most noise sources are measured in terms of intensity or strength of the sound field. The standard unit of one decibel (dB) is the amount of sound which is just audible to the average human. The decibel scale is somewhat misleading because it is logarithmic rather than linear. For example, a noise source measuring 70 dB is 10 times as loud as a source measuring 60 dB and 100 times as loud as a source reading 50 dB. Noise may be generally related to industrial society where heavy machineries like, motor vehicles and aircraft have become everyday items. Noise pollution is generally more intense in the work environment than in the general environment. The ambient noise increased is with an average of one dB per year during the 1980s. Today, the average background of noise in a typical home is between 40 and 50 decibels. Some examples of high-level sources in the environment are heavy trucks (90 dB at 15 m/50 ft), freight trains (75 dB at 15 m/50 ft), and air conditioning (60 dB at 6 m/20 ft).

The most recognised measurable physiological effect of the noise pollution is the damage to hearing which may be either partially or permanent and may cause disruption of normal activities. However, the effect is variable, depending upon individual susceptibility and duration of exposure, nature of noise and time distribution of exposure such as steady or intermittent. On an average, an individual will experience a threshold shift i.e., a shift in an individual's upper limit of sound detect ability, when exposed to noise levels of 75 to 80 dB for several hours. This will end only several hours once the source of noise pollution is removed. However, a second physiologically important level is the threshold of pain at which even the short-term exposure will cause physical pain i.e., 130 dB to 140 dB. At this level, any noise sustained level will cause a permanent threshold shift or permanent partial hearing loss. At the uppermost level of noise (greater than 150 dB), even a single short-term blast may cause traumatic hearing loss and physical damage to the inside ear.

Picture: Noise Pollution

There is very little heard information available on the psychological side effects of increased noise levels. Various researchers attribute increased irritability, lower productivity, decreased tolerance level, increased incidence of ulcers, migraine headaches, fatigue, and allergic responses to continued exposures to high-level noises in the workplace and the general environment.

Mitigation of Noise pollution: Reducing noise pollution by muffling the sounds at the source is one of the best methods in industry and for urban living. Protective equipment is generally mandatory when noise levels exceed 85 dB(A) in industry. Creation of green cover adjacent to municipal roads and in mines is the way to mitigate noise pollution. It has been observed that noise level reduces by 10 decibels every 10 m wide green belt development. Apart from this, redesigning industrial equipment, shock mounting assemblies and physical barriers in the workplace are also for reduction and exposure of unwanted industrial noise.

Noise pollution on highway can be mitigated by constructing noise barriers. Tree plantation around houses can also act as effective noise barriers. Artificial noise barriers are solid obstructions built between the highway and the residential areas along a highway. They block significant portion of noise produced by passing vehicles on a highway. Effective noise barriers typically reduce noise levels by as much as half or more. The construction of noise barrier may be built in the form of earth mounds and creation of vertical wall along the highways for blockage of sound generated by heavy vehicles. Creation of greenbelt in the space between the residences and highways also reduces the noise nuisance.

Pollution Control Boards and Measures to Control Pollution

The Central Pollution Control Board (CPCB) was constituted on 22nd September 1974 as Central Board for Prevention and Control of Water Pollution (CBPCWP) under the provisions of The Water (Prevention & Control of Pollution) Act, 1974, and later under Water (Prevention & Control of Pollution) Amendment Act 1988. Its name was amended as Central Pollution Control Board. The main functions of CPCB, as spelt out in The Water (Prevention and Control of Pollution) Act, 1974, and The Air (Prevention and Control of Pollution) Act, 1981, are:

- To promote streams' cleanliness and of wells in different areas of the States through prevention, control and abatement of water pollution.
- To improve air quality and to prevent, control or abate air pollution in the country.

The Central Pollution Control Board plays significant role in controlling pollution by generating necessary data, providing scientific information, rendering technical inputs for formation of national policies and programmes, training and development of manpower, through activities for promoting awareness at different levels of the Government and Public at large. The Central Board has highlighted the thrust areas requiring immediate attention and assisted government to formulate National Plans and to execute them appropriately.

Functions of the Central Board

- To advise and suggest the Central Government on any matter concerning prevention and control of water and air pollution and improvement of the quality of air;
- Plan and cause to be executed as a nation-wide programme for the prevention, control or abatement of water and air pollution;
- Co-ordinate the activities of the State Boards and resolve disputes among them;
- To provide technical assistance and guidance to the State Boards and carry out activities and sponsor investigations and research relating to problems of water and air pollution, and for their prevention, control or abatement;
- To plan and organise training programmes for persons engaged in it for prevention and control of water and air pollution;
- To organise through mass media, a comprehensive mass awareness programme on prevention and control of water and air pollution;
- To collect, compile and publish technical and statistical data relating to water and air pollution and the measures devised for their effective prevention and control;

- To prepare manuals, codes and guidelines relating to the treatment and disposal of sewage waste and trade effluents as well as for stack gas cleaning devices, stacks and ducts;
- To disseminate valuable information in respect of matters relating to water and air pollution and their prevention and control;
- To lay down and modify in consultation with the State Governments concerned, the standards for stream or well, and lay down standards for the quality of air; and
- To perform such other functions whenever assigned and prescribed by the Government of India.

We have seen in this chapter that environmental degradation is a process through which the natural environment is compromised in some way, by reducing biological diversity and the general health of the environment. This process can be entirely natural in origin, or it can be accelerated or caused by human activities. Many international organisations recognise environmental degradation as one of the major threats facing the planet, since humans have only been given one Earth to work with, and if the environment becomes irreparably compromised, it could mean the end of human existence.

There are numerous ways in which environmental degradation can work. In a classic case, resources simply become depleted. All-natural resources like air, water and soil are vulnerable to depletion through overexploitation and other natural resources like minerals and oil deposits. Habitat pressures which force animals into a small area can also contribute to resource depletion, as the animals consume a high volume of material in a small area.

Pollution is another major cause of natural environmental degradation. When the environment becomes severely polluted it means that hazardous toxic substances have rendered it unhealthy. Pollution can come from numerous sources like, vehicle emissions, agricultural runoff, chemical releases from big factories and poorly managed harvesting of natural resources. In some cases, pollution may be reversible with costly environmental remediation measures, and in other instances, it may take decades or even centuries for the environment to cope with the pollution.

It is evident from the study that environment is being degraded day by day by human being. In case adequate steps are not taken to prevent environmental pollution and to improve the quality of life by providing more essential measures, the life of the living people may become more miserable which may be the cause of health hazards and worst devastation. To achieve this, population must be controlled. Urgent attention should be given to reduce the environmental pollution through mandatory standards and regulation. Improved technologies should be developed for waste collection, treatment, and disposal in order to ensure proper solid waste management.

Present study indicates that maintenance of high quality of life in present environment requires the protection of environmental quality leading towards sustainable development. Serious attention should be given to the need for improving natural environmental condition, and promote efficiency in resource use.

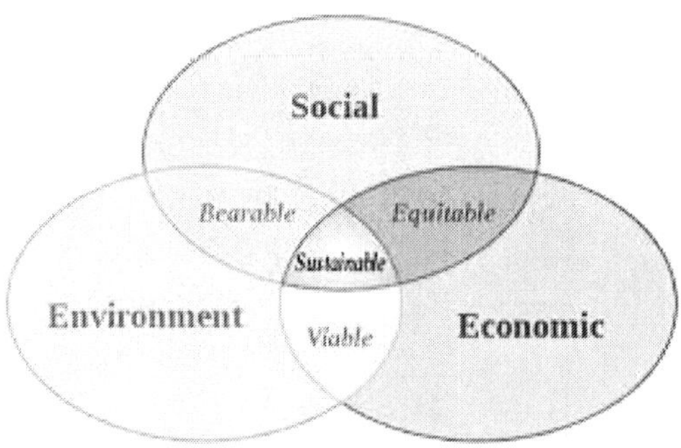

Picture: Sustainable Development

We are living in a rapidly changing global community, in a fast developing, highly diverse country. The environmental issues which were salient but as of now they may evolve over time, and new ones may take their place. Scientific understanding of environmental matters would increase rapidly. Changes in economic structure, technologies, resource availability, in each case like, local, national as well as global, are likely, as are evolution of global environmental regimes, and norms arising from jurisprudence.

The approach towards environmental protection now needs to be more focused, integrated and inclusive. It must consider all stakeholders-directly or indirectly involved with the system.

Chapter - 4

Environmental Planning

Environmental Planning is said to be a facilitating decision process and to carry out development with due consideration given to the natural environmental, social, political, economic and governance factors and provides an overall framework to achieve sustainable outcomes.

When communities, cities, states and countries become more aware and concerned about the distribution of their natural resources the environmental planning becomes increasingly critical. However, the desirable goal of environmental planning is to determine the designs of cities and towns. The planning focuses on how to achieve community development through sustainable development and use of natural resources in a way that it is good for the ecosystem and the general population.

The concerns for planners are not only about the environmental damage but also about strains on transportation, diminishing natural resources, and many other problems that plague cities around the world.

All environmental planners must have an in-depth knowledge of economics, geography, environmental science, political science, engineering, and demography. However, issues of sustainability create a significant problem for many urban cities and regions. But environmental planners work to provide solutions to these problems. Climate change, urban sprawl, deforestation and air pollution may have an adverse impact on the natural environment, but environmental planning focuses on how such problems can be addressed.

Environmental planners also search and explore the nature of intricate relationship between people and its environment. They, however, determine how routine activities impact on the environment instead of a deadly one. They determine how a community can change its norms and values with respect to the surrounding environment by evaluating land use, infrastructure, and the community's natural resources. Environmental planning is concerned more with increasing the quality of life of human beings and environment.

Environmental planning also concerns itself with decision-making processes where they are required for managing relationships that exist within and between natural systems and human systems. Environmental planning strives to manage these processes in an effective, orderly, transparent and equitable manner for the benefit of all constituents within such systems for the present and for the future. Today, the Environmental planning practices are the result of continuous refinement and expansion of the scope of such decision-making processes. Some of the main elements of present-day environmental planning are:

- Social and economic development
- Urban development
- Regional development
- Natural resource management and integrated land use
- Infrastructure systems
- Governance frameworks

Thus, the environmental planning assesses and encompasses the areas like, land use, socio-economics, transportation, economic and housing characteristics, air pollution, noise pollution and the wetlands, habitat of the many endangered species, flood zones susceptibility, coastal zones erosion, and visual studies among others and is referred to as an Integrated environmental planning assessment.

In India, The Ministry of Environment and Forests is the nodal agency for the formulation of planning, promotion and supervising the implementation of various environmental programmes. Through its proper policy statement released in June 1992 it had set up the task to ensure sustainable and equitable use of the environmental natural resources for meeting out the basic needs of the present and future generations without the damage to the natural environment.

The Ministry has already initiated legislative and regulatory measures aimed at the preservation and protection of environment. Some of these include: Air (Prevention and Control of Pollution) Act, 1981; the Water (Prevention and Control of Pollution) Act, 1974; the Environment (Protection) Act, 1986; the Public Liability Insurance Act, 1955; the National Environment Appellate Authority Act, 1997; the Wildlife Protection Act, 1972 and the Forest (Con-servation) Act, 1980. Besides these legislative measures, a National Conservation Strategy and Policy Statement on Environment and Development, 1992; the National Forest Policy, 1988 and a Policy Statement on Abatement of Pollution, 1992 have also been evolved.

(1) Pollution Control: The Central Pollution Control Board (CPCB) has, however, been constituted for assessment, monitoring and control of water and air pollution.

The Pollution Board has recognised 17 categories of heavily polluting industries which include cement, thermal power plants, distilleries, sugar factories, chemical fertilisers, integrated iron and steel, oil refineries, paper and pulp, petro-chemicals plant, pesticides, tanneries, basic drugs and pharmaceuticals factories, dye and dye intermediates, caustic soda, zinc smelter, copper smelter and aluminum smelter. Out of a total of 2,155 units recognised so far under these categories, 1,877 units have installed pollution control devices. The Board has also however, identified 13 extremely polluted rivers of India which include the Sabarmati river between Ahmadabad and Vautha, The Yamuna river between Delhi and its confluence with Chambal, The Subarnarekha river between Hathidam and Bahragara, The Godavari river between Nashik and Nanded, The Krishna river between Karad and Sangli, The Damodar river between Dhanbad and Haldia, The Gomati river between Lucknow and its confluence with Ganga, The Kali between Modinagar and its confluence with Ganga, The Shipra river in the city limits of Ujjain, The Hindon river between Saharanpur and its confluence with Yamuna, The

Ganga river between Kanpur and Farakka, The Khan in the city limits of Indore, and The Chambal. The National River Conservation Plan covers 152 towns along 27 inter-state rivers in 16 states. Under this Governments' Action Plan, water pollution abatement works are being taken up in almost 57 towns. A total of 215 major schemes of pollution abatement have been approved under this plan. A proposal for three lakes, namely, Powai (Maharashtra), Ooty and Kodaikanal (Tamil Nadu) were approved under the National Lake Conservation Plan (NLCP).

There are twenty-two critically polluted areas which have been recognised in the country for special attention on pollution abatement. These areas are for example, Vapi (Gujarat), Singrauli (Uttar Pradesh), Korba (Chhattisgarh), Ratlam and Nagda (M.P.), Digboi (Assam), Talcher (Odisha), Bhadravati (Karnataka), Haora (W. Bengal), Dhanbad (Jharkhand), Pali and Jodhpur (Rajasthan), Manali and North Arcot (Tamil Nadu), Vishakhapatnam and Patancheru (Andhra Pradesh), Chembur (Maharashtra), Najafgarh (Delhi), Govindgarh (Punjab), Udyog Mandal (Kerala), and Parwanoo and Kala Amb (Himachal Pradesh). There has been constituted an Eco Task Force to work in environmentally degraded areas. This scheme has been especially involved to use the services of ex-service men.

(2) Environmental Impact Assessment: The programme of Environmental Impact Assessment (EIA) has been introduced in 1978. A notification issued in January 1994 makes EIA statutory for 29 categories of development projects under various sectors such as industrial, mining, irrigation, power, transport, tourism, communication, etc. Recently, one more item Meta Amino Phenyl has been added to this list.

The Ministry of Environment, Forest and Climate Change (MoEF & CC) has published the draft Environment Impact Assessment (EIA) Notification 2020, with the intention of replacing the existing EIA Notification, 2006 under the Environment (Protection) Act, 1986. An EIA makes a scientific estimate of the likely impacts of a project, such as a mine, irrigation dam, industrial unit or waste treatment plant. There is also a provision for public consultation in the rules, including a public hearing at which the local community and interested persons can give opinions and raise objections, based on the draft EIA report prepared by experts for the project.

(3) Biosphere Reserves: Thirteen biosphere reserves have been set up in different parts of the country to preserve the genetic diversity and integrity of plants, animals and micro-organisms. These include: Nilgiri Biosphere Reserve in Kerala, Nanda Devi Biosphere Reserve in Uttarakhand, Nokrek Biosphere Reserve in Meghalaya, Great Nicobar Biosphere Reserve in Andman and Nicobar, Gulf of Mannar, Manas Biosphere Reserve in Assam, Sunderbans Biosphere Reserve in West Bengal, Similipal Biosphere Reserve in Odisha, Dibru Daikhowa Biosphere Reserve, Dehong Deband Biosphere Reserve in Arunachal Pradesh, Panchmarhi Biosphere Reserve in Madhya Pradesh, Kanchanjanga in Assam and Agasthyamalai Biosphere Reserve in Tami Nadu. Amongst these four, namely Nilgiri, Sunderbans, Gulf of Mannar and Nanda Devi (Valley of Flowers), have been recognised on World Network of Biosphere Reserves by the UNESCO.

(4) Biological Diversity: Biological diversity has major consumptive economic value in food, agriculture, medicine and industry. It also maintains the ecology and continucs evolutionary

Tiger Reserve

process. India is one of the major and most important nations of 17 mega diverse countries which together possess 60 to 70 percent of the world's biodiversity. From the 70 percent of the total geographical area surveyed so far, about 16,000 plant species and 81,000 animal species have been identified. India became a member to this International Convention on Biological Diversity in May 1994.

The National Policy and Action Strategy on Biodiversity seek to consolidate the on-going efforts to conserve and sustainable use of biological diversity and to establish a proper policy and programme for the same purpose. In India, it was released by the Ministry of Environment and Forests on 6 January, 2000. It aims at preserving and conserving biodiversity through a network of protected areas

Biodiversity

including national parks, biosphere reserves, marine reserves, sanctuaries gene conservation centers, wetlands, coral reefs and such other natural habitats of biodiversity.

It mainly focuses on the: (i) conservation of fauna and flora which help in the reclamation of wastelands and revival of biological capacities of the land, (ii) protection of domesticated species or varieties of plants and animals in order to conserve indigenous genetic diversity, and (iii) development of methodologies to multiply numerous breeds and conserve the threatened and endangered species through modern techniques of tissue culture and bio-technology. Parliament has recently passed Bio Diversity Act 2002 to protect country's biodiversity and check bio-piracy.

(5) Wildlife Protection: The National Wildlife Action Plan provides the framework of strategy for the conservation of wildlife. Under the new wildlife Action Plan (2002- 2016), the wildlife protected area network comprises 92 national parks and 590 sanctuaries covering an area of 1.57 lakh sq. km.

Picture: Wildlife

The Wildlife (Protection) Act, 1972 adopted by all states except Jammu and Kashmir (which has its own Act), governs wildlife conservation and protection of endangered species. Under Project Tiger (launched on 1 April, 1973), 28 Tiger Reserves have been set up in 17 states covering an area of 37,761 sq. km. Similarly, the Project Elephant (launched in February, 1992) is being implemented in

17 states. The research programmes in wildlife are carried out by the Wildlife Institute of India, Dehradun and the Salim Ali Centre for Ornithology and Natural History, Coimbatore.

(6) Afforestation: The National Afforestation and Eco-Development Board (NAEB) was created in 1992 and was assigned the task of promoting afforestation, tree plantation and ecological restoration and eco-development activities in the country with special attention to degraded forest areas and ecologically fragile areas like the Western Himalayas, the Aravallis, Western Ghats, etc.

The NAEB plans to carry out its responsible activities through various schemes like, the Integrated Afforestation and Eco-development Projects (IAEPs) and areas-oriented fuel wood and fodder projects, non-timber forest produce scheme including medicinal plants, aerial seeding, seed development, technology extension, grants-in-aid to voluntary agencies, etc. It has also launched programmes of Joint Forest Management (JFM), Samanvit Gram Vanikaran Samriddhi Yojana (SGVSY), Coastal Shelter belt Plantation Programme (CSPP) and bamboo and medicinal plantation projects.

(7) International Co-operation: The Ministry of Environment and Forests functions as nodal agency for United Nations Environment Programme (UNEP), South Asia Cooperation Environment Programme International Centre for Integrated Mountain Development (ICIMOD), International Union for Conservation of Nature and Natural Resources (IUCN) and various other international agencies, regional bodies and multilateral institutions. It participates in interna-tional conventions and handles bilateral issues and matters pertaining to multilateral and regional bodies.

(8) Ozone Cell: India accorded to the Montreal Protocol along with its London Amendment on Ozone Depleting Substances (ODS) in 1992. To meet the country's commitment on ODS an Ozone Cell has been established in India. This Cell publishes a bi-monthly news-letter on ozone issues. Custom/excise duty exemption is allowed on ODS phase-out projects and on the import of non-ODS technologies. The Ozone Depleting Substances Regulation and Control Rules, 2000 ensures compliance of the Montreal Protocol.

(9) Environmental Information System: The Environmental Information System (ENVIS) was established in 1982 for the collection, collation, storage, retrieval and dissemination of environmental information at local, regional and national level. It consists of 25 subject-oriented centers set up in various institutions or organisations of the country in priority areas of the environmental study. It also brings out a quarterly journal, i.e., Paryavaran Abstracts, containing information about environmental research in the Indian context. It is also publishing a bi-monthly newsletter, i.e., Environment News. The ENVIS has been designated as National Focal Point (NFP) and Regional Service Centre (RSC) for South Asia sub-regional countries by INFOTERRA, a global information system on environment, of United Nations Environment Programme (UNEP).

(10) Environmental Education: Priority is accorded by the Ministry of Environment and Forests to promote environmental education, create environmental awareness among various age groups of people to disseminate information through ENVIS. A major initiative to include environmental education as a separate and compulsory subject in the education curricula has been taken by the Ministry at all levels of formal education, i.e. secondary, senior secondary and tertiary levels. The Ministry also accord priority for the promotion of non-formal environmental education and creation of awareness among all sections of the society. It organises seminars/symposia/workshops, training programmes, National Green Corps (NGC), eco-clubs, audio-visual shows, etc. *World Environment Day* (WED) is celebrated every year on 5th June and is the United Nations' principal vehicle for encouraging awareness and action for the protection of the environment. First held in 1974, it has been a platform for raising awareness on environmental issue such as marine pollution, human overpopulation, global warming, sustainable consumption and wildlife crime. Similarly, a National Environmental Campaign (NEAC) is also organised every year.

Moreover, seven centers at Dhanbad, Bangalore, Ahmadabad, Chennai, Coimbatore, Delhi and Thiruvananthapuram have been established by the Governments' Ministry to strengthen awareness, research and training programmes in priority areas of the environmental

Tree Plantation

science and management. The National Museum of Natural History (NMNH), New Delhi (1978) is concerned for the promotion of non-formal education in the area of environment and conservation. It has also established three regional museums at Mysore, Bhopal and Bhubaneswar. Various fellowships and awards have been instituted to promote environmen-tal education and awareness.

Afforestation

We are living in the era of decreasing natural resources and environmental deterioration. Global biodiversity is declining at accelerating rate. Urbanisation, industrialisation and other human activities have consequences in deforestation and environmental pollution causing severe threat to the natural environment. It contains many important and valuable plants from scientific point of view, apart from the economically viable ones. Now the realisation about environmental degradation is spread all over the world that survival of mankind is not possible without forests, which is an important

Afforestation

part of the ecosystem of our planet earth. Forests with their plenty of flora and fauna are rich sources of gene pool. So, conservation biologists have increased efforts to understand its degradation and encourage its conservation. However, genetic conservation was started with biosphere reserves, sanctuaries and national parks all over the world as a part of the conservation strategy.

The significance of preserving natural diversity is to maintain ecological balance, viable economic use of species and genetic material for evolving new varieties in agriculture, horticulture, veterinary and medical fields and proper maintenance of life system and preserve aesthetic and religious values. It also seeks to know the socio-economic value of a particular area and to preserve its culture and nature. This necessitates making inventory of diversity of the country and the monitoring. The proximate causes of biodiversity loss may be anthropological, biological, social, economic or political. However, we cannot afford to lose the biological diversity of their direct and indirect benefit. Evaluation of soil has become important due to worldwide problem of conserving biological diversity. Although soil is formed due to the result of weathering of parent rock, effect of climate, topography, plants, animals and age of land forms various factors affect the formation of the soil in many ways. The close relationships between geology, soil and vegetation are clearly visible by the effect shown by parent material and strong biological activity on soil formation and characteristics. Geological studies have significant importance in forestry where tree growth lasts over a long period and depends to a large extent on the minerals as a source of nutrients in the soil. However, the knowledge of mineralogical behaviour of soils at good natural sites and also at degraded sites opens the possibilities of optimal management inputs to augment production of the biomass from good site as well as from degraded site after suitable amelioration. The fertility potential of growing species in the present intensified programme of raising large scale plantation mainly depends on the mineralogical composition of the soil. The underlying parent material plays a vital role in determining the success or other-wise of the plantations especially over a number of rotations in a given year.

Environmental Planning

Geological studies have been very useful in understanding the ecological status of forest growth and in identifying various problems like deterioration in growth, quality, loss of vigour, mortality etc. in forest crops which are often caused by nutrient deficiency and other soil factors, some of which are related to mineralogical composition. Diagnostic supports to determine the inter-relationship between geology, soil and vegetation and to work out potential productivity of soil as a useful tool for sustainable management of degraded sites. Soil is being enriched through nutrient contribution from minerals. Such evaluation is helpful for the managers and land users to have a thorough knowledge about the content and nature of minerals present in the soil in diagnosing the fertility status and other soil-plant-parent material relationship in forestry. It is useful to work out proper requirement of nutrients for a particular species for a sustainable activity on such sites.

To implement and enhance the potential use of soil mineralogical evaluation some guidelines are however, proposed for eco-rehabilitation of natural forest sites as well as degraded land. A detailed survey of soil and vegetation should be carried out and site matched species as per mineralogical studies should be identified and planted. A holistic study of different geological parameters of the sites should be conducted. Mineralogical evaluation should be carried out which are occurring under different conditions of soil, climate and geology to bring out suitable remedial measures for sustainable development and afforestation.

The concern for environmental protection got a boost when Forest Conservation Act came into force in 1980. Compensatory afforestation got more systematic with the creation of Compensatory Afforestation Management and Planning Authority (CAMPA) in April 2004. The CAMPA is yet to get fully activated to produce good results and it again depends upon the states to prepare and execute viable schemes for the development of forests, ensuring plantation of trees on lands allotted for compensatory afforestation.

There is world-wide concern about environment protection and the evolution of the concept of Sustainable Development which may be useful in achieving the objectives of holding 33% of forest cover in the country. The sustained use of the involved land for societal needs and economic gains is the watch word for future development. The present minerals came into the existence much prior to the advent of plants and animals on the earth. The forest wealth and the mineral resources share a common habitat and the mineral exploitation interferes with the forest growth, rather it destroys it completely. The mining is thus an environmentally unfriendly industry. It is permitted in the name of industrial development, a more important tool for the modern civilisation. The industry brings wealth and jobs to millions and results in the national prosperity. The minerals will be exhausted in the coming years and the mined-out area will get desolated and unfit for further any societal activity. Recently, Mine Closure plan had been made a responsibility of the mining company and there is a financial provision also.

However, the available legislative framework and the societal norms concern are two very important pillars which may ensure the restoration of mined out areas to near normal conditions. It will be very helpful if the sustained land use and ensuring equally profitable gains to the society help to a great extent in erasing the ill effects of mining. The profit motive will sustain the society and provide the future generations with the means of livelihood.

Current-Scenario

The afforestation currently worked upon and done in the past has helped in increasing the tree cover. The mined-out areas look green. Fast growing plant species had been planted. The resultant forest is thus a green patch of trees of low economic value. They are good for fuel, fodder and stock for paper and pulp industry. Due to this reason the forests in our economy contribute only 1.3% of the GDP. It is the root cause of abject poverty of people living in the forests and its periphery. Tribal and farmers who constitute 70% of our population live in very low level of subsistence. Thus, there is a great need to plant valuable trees.

According to the 2019 report, the total forest cover of the country is 712,249 square kilometers (21.67 percent of India's total geographical area) slightly up from 708,273 sq. km (21.54 percent) in 2017. The tree cover of the country is 95,027 sq. km (2.89 percent of the total area) again slightly up from 93,815 sq. km. (2.85 percent) in 2017.

The rapid increase in the depletion of the trees reduces the ground water also. This affects the growth of other trees and even affects the drinking water resources for the people living in the forests. According to the MOEF, about 200 million people depend on forests besides their cattle. The MOEF has a vast afforestation program. They are eyeing the waste land also for afforestation as the vacant land is decreasing within the forest areas for compensatory afforestation.

These are very encouraging to grow more trees and to increase the forest cover. The current efforts are again directed towards the plantation of fast-growing varieties like, mulberry, jatropa and medicinal plants. They are essential for the society and may add some value to the forests in the years to come. Private entrepreneurs may also be involved to help in raising plantation on degraded forests. States are being encouraged to prepare plantation schemes to help in the efforts of forests development. It is the right time to rethink in our strategies for future developments.

Outline-of-New-Strategy

It is a well-known fact that our aim is economic development and increasing the earnings of the country men as a whole. The mining activity, as long as it goes on, compensates the people around to a great extent and they live a good life. When the mine closes the local people get affected immediately. There is thus a great need to help these persons to have alternative means of livelihood. The afforestation programme should thus aim at value addition to the planted trees and looking for new avenues for employment. The following points may be useful:

1. Valuable timber trees like teak, rosewood and sandalwood are planted.
2. Fruit trees plantation may be encouraged.
3. Orchards and gardens are created.

4. Efforts are made to develop eco-tourism sites.
5. Hill stations are developed as after independence no hill station has been created.

The growing valuable trees may take long time to develop to the size for use. They can be grown on crop pattern. All the regions of the country grow specific type of trees. Trees with valuable wood can be selected and planted while doing afforestation on any land available for the purpose. Sandalwood, the most valuable wood, grows in many areas in Deccan plateau, and is considered as local specie. There are good prospects of growing sandalwood in and around the mines in Bellary-Hospet area. Teak can be grown in the forest areas of Madhya Pradesh, Chhattisgarh, Jharkhand and many states in Deccan area. The plantation of these trees will help in ensuring the availability of good quality timber in future.

Fruits are now considered a major part of food item in Indian homes. Good qualities of fruits have become a significant export item for earning good returns to the farmers. Emerging markets for fruit business are getting streamlined due to the entry of retailers and they are keen to establish processing and marketing establishments. It is a cash crop and farmers are also taking interest in growing fruits. Fruit based industry may provide more jobs to the people in and around forests.

There is possibility of creating gardens and orchards in mined out areas. Mined out mine benches may be converted to terrace farms for growing vegetables and flowers. The benches are provided with soil cover to support vegetation. Flowers have a very important emerging market with export possibilities. Terraces are good landform for inducting irrigation network working on gravity principle.

According to MOEF, medicinal plant caters to the needs of 80% of Ayurvedic, 46% of Unani and 33% of Allopathic medicines. Out of 47,000 plant species in India, 15,000 are of medicinal values. According to Ministry of Ayush, Government of India, the major increase has been recorded in export value which has increased from 345.80 crore in 2005-06 to 3211 crore in 2014-15, registering a nine-fold increase in during last decade. Govt. of India has constituted

The National Medicinal Plants Board (NMPB). It will be very appropriate if the afforestation programmes include plantation of medicinal plants in large numbers. NMPB has a mandate to develop this sector and to help in removing the bottlenecks. The board will also work as a think tank and data bank.

Areas around mines may sometimes be scenic beauty spots. Such spots are numerous and may be projected and developed. The mine as long as it is productive, attracts people connected with mining. Awareness of the people towards forest preservation is growing. People are curious to know about forests, desirous of interaction with tribal and interested in learning crafts living styles of tribal. Ecotourism can easily be developed in mining areas as there is already some infrastructure and much more can be developed at low cost. It will provide employment to the locals and may encourage selling of forest products and crafts. People visiting forest areas may act as eyes and ears of the authorities and will eventually help in forest and wildlife conservation. The concept is now evolving and societal and administrative mechanism is under development. State Tourism Departments may help in popularising ecotourism and should encourage tourist traffic.

After independence tourism to hill stations has grown and many flocks to the popular hill resorts. These resorts are unable to cope up with the increasing demand of the coming people for tourism. There is great shortage of accommodation, water, parking and commercial space. The Deccan plateau flanked by Eastern and Western Ghats has numerous mineral bearing hillocks where mining activities are going on. The mine closure idea may include the creation of a mined-out areas which may provide space for parks and gardens, water bodies, infrastructure and housing. In this regard, the mining company, the state govt. and the Tourism Department may join hands together. There are various mines in the region where the working heights generally vary between 800 to 1200 metres. The temperatures range between 15 to 35 degrees centigrade. There are numerous established hill stations like, Mount Abu 1220 M, Anantagiri 600-900 M, Horsely Hills 1265 M, Matheran 800 M, Panchgani 1100 M, Khandala 625 M, Lonavala 1150 M and Chikaldara 1120 M. Various iron and manganese ores mines in Deccan can be developed as a hill station.

However, the increasing environmental awareness and closure of mine legislation may be very helpful in encouraging for the development of new hill stations. It is quite possible that mining may be transformed to create proper landscape, water bodies and gardens to help in creating a hill station after the closing of mining operations. It is an important idea and the state governments may include such places in their development schemes. There are already plans to convert Kudrumukh mines to an important hill resort.

Developmental-Philosophy

Awareness for conservation is new as well as the legal framework. Many unresolved issues are there such as the jurisdiction of states and the central government. Issues related to Tribal are within the jurisdiction of Ministry of Tribal Welfare. One important issue is, "once a forest always a forest". If we think about developing forests, many rules related to forests may come in the way. Broadly no non-forest activity is permitted in a forest area unless a proper permission is obtained. Once the activity is over, the land returns to the forest department. The strategies suggested above may change the land use. How far this may be possible is a matter to be debated and broadly acceptable way out to be evolved.

If we are intended to develop orchards, flower beds and fruit tree groves, the high valuable trees and medicinal plants may have to obtain permissions for cultivation. This may change the land use forever. How to be allowed this for use is yet to be resolved? There may be requirement of high level of securities for the valuable plantations. The present level of security in the forests is rather very poor. However, the growing economic activity may need personal as well as material safety. Presently our forests are very unsafe because poachers and timber mafia roam freely in the forests. The forest cover is gradually declining. There is thus a need to evolve appropriate mechanism before we adopt new strategies. Currently forests are environmental needs and the economics of land use has not yet been considered a forest specific activity.

Human development needs put pressure on the forests and lot of forest areas are cleared to provide lands for societal needs. Forest development and the development needs can be dovetailed to achieve both. Forest development related laws can be amended to permit human settlements in the forests and be permitted to start the activities suggested above.

There is a need for in-depth study of the pros and cons of the new strategy so that both the objectives of forest conservation and societal need are fulfilled. This will need a new legal framework which can be evolved after mutual consultations amongst the stake holders.

Afforestation with value addition may help in increasing the incomes of the people living in the forests. A synergy between forest conservation and appropriate industrialisation of forests will certainly help in developing employment opportunities for people living in and around the forests. Such people comprise of 70% of our total population. They subsist on wages between Rs 20 to Rs 40 per day. The present 1.3% of GDP accrued from the forests can be increased many times with not much of investment as the activities suggested may run concurrently with the mining and the other related afforestation programmes. Mining is an important location for specific industry and cannot be done anywhere else. Unfortunately, our mineral wealth is predominantly scattered in forested areas. Lack of infrastructural development of forest and peripheral areas creates large scale unemployment and giving rise to social conflict and unavoidable tensions. This needs urgent attention and a need to evolve a mechanism to achieve enrichment of forests.

Water Conservation

"When well is dry we know the value of water"

Benjamin Franklin.

Conserving water has become a prime environmental concern. Clean water is becoming increasingly scarce globally. With deforestation, surface run-off increases and the sub-soil water table drops as water has no time to seep slowly into the ground once the vegetation is cleared. As many areas depend on wells, it has become necessary to go on digging deeper and deeper wells. This adds to the further cost and depletes underground stored water. This could take many years to recharge even if the present rate of extinction is checked, which seems hardly possible in most situations.

As deforestation and desertification increases due to extensive change in land use patterns, the once-perennial rivers are increasingly becoming seasonal. In various areas, the small streams run by soon after the monsoon as the water table declines further and further below the surface. To this adds the serious problems caused by rapid surface flow of water during the rains, which leads to extensive floods with loss of human and animal life and property.

When we waste water, we generally do not realise the importance of it that affects the lives of all of us in various ways. Water has to be used judiciously and equitably and fairly distributed so that household use, agricultural and industry all get a share of the water. Its overexploitation and misuse due to various activities that waste water and causes pollution has led to a serious shortage of potable drinking water. Thus, water conservation is linked closely with overall human well-being.

Picture: Water conservation

Even various religious texts and epics give a good insight into the water storage and conservation systems that were prevailed in those days. Over the many years, the increasing population and growing industrialisation and expanding agriculture have increased the demand for water. Efforts are being made to collect water by building dams and reservoirs and digging wells; some countries have also tried to recycle and desalinate (remove salts) water. Water conservation has become need of the hour. The idea of ground water recharging by harvesting rainwater is gaining importance in various cities. In the forest's areas, water seeps gently into the ground as vegetation breaks the fall. This groundwater in turn feeds wells, lakes, and rivers. Protecting forests means protecting water catchments. In ancient India, people believed that forests were the 'mothers' of rivers and worshipped the sources of these water bodies.

Some Ancient Indian methods of water conservation

The Indus Valley Civilisation flourished along the banks of the river Indus. Other parts of western and northern India about 5,000 years ago had one of the most sophisticated urban water supply and sewage systems in the world. The fact, the people were well familiar with hygiene and can be evidenced from the covered drains running beneath the streets of the ruins at both Mohanjodaro and Harappa. Another classical example is the well-planned city of Dholavira, on Khadir Bet, a low plateau in the Rann in Gujarat. One of the oldest waters harvesting systems is found about 130 km from Pune in the Western Ghats. However, a large number of tanks were cut in the rocks to provide drinking water to tradesmen who used to travel along this ancient trade route. Each fort in the area had its own water harvesting and storage system in the form of rock-cut cisterns, ponds, tanks and wells that are still in use today. Moreover, a large number of forts like Raigad, had tanks that supplied water. In ancient times, houses in parts of western Rajasthan were built so that each had a system of rooftop water harvesting. Rainwater from these rooftops was directed into underground tanks. This system can be seen even today in all the forts, palaces and houses of this region. Underground baked earthen pipes and tunnels to maintain the flow of water and to transport it to distant places, are still in operation at Burhanpur in Madhya Pradesh, Golkunda and Bijapur in Karnataka, and Aurangabad in Maharashtra.

Rainwater-harvesting

'As our world faces severe water shortages, it counts every drop of water and we can use it efficiently becomes of great value'. One method is to manage rainwater in such a way that it is used at the source. If as much water as possible is collected and stored, this can be used once the rainy season is over. In various parts of the world especially in severely dry areas this has been traditionally practiced.

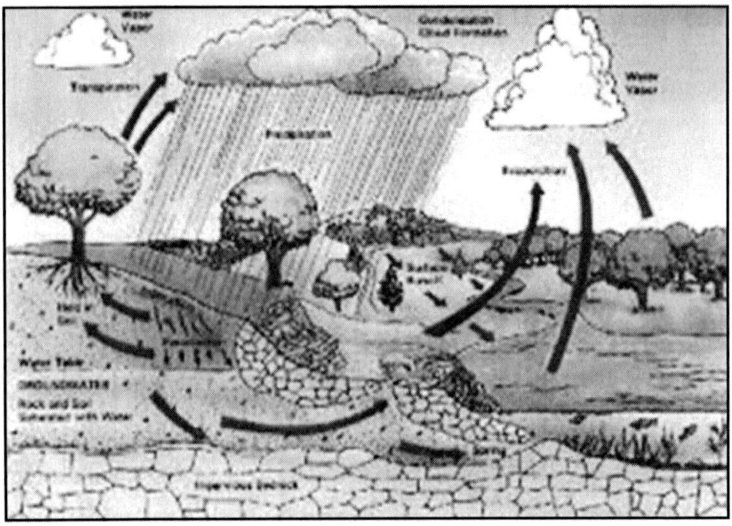

Hydrological Cycle

However, the stored water has to be kept pollution-free and clean so that it can be used as drinking water. Stored water can grow algae and zooplankton (microscopic animals). This can be pathogenic and cause infectious. Thus, keeping the water uncontaminated is of great importance. In urban areas, the construction of houses, footpaths and roads has left little exposed earth for water to soak in. In parts of the rural areas of India, floodwater quickly flows to the rivers, which then dry up soon after the rains stop. If this water can be held back, it can seep into the ground and recharge the groundwater supply.

This has become a very significant method of conserving and storing water especially in the urban areas. Rainwater harvesting is essentially a process of collecting rainwater on the roofs of building and storing it underground for later use. Not only does this recharging arrest groundwater depletion, it also raises the declining water table and can help augment water supply. Today, rainwater harvesting and artificial recharging are becoming very popular issues. It is essential to stop the decline of groundwater levels, arrest sea-water ingress, i.e. prevent sea-water from moving landward, and conserve surface water run-off during the rainy season.

Town planners and civic authority in many cities in India are introducing bylaws making rainwater harvesting compulsory in all new structures. No water or sewage connection would be given if a new building did not have provisions for rainwater harvesting. Such rules should also be implemented in all the other cities to ensure a rise in the groundwater level. Realising the importance of recharging groundwater, the CGWB (Central Ground Water Board) is taking major steps to encourage it through rainwater harvesting in the capital and major cities and elsewhere. Large numbers of government buildings have been asked to go in for water harvesting in Delhi and other cities of India.

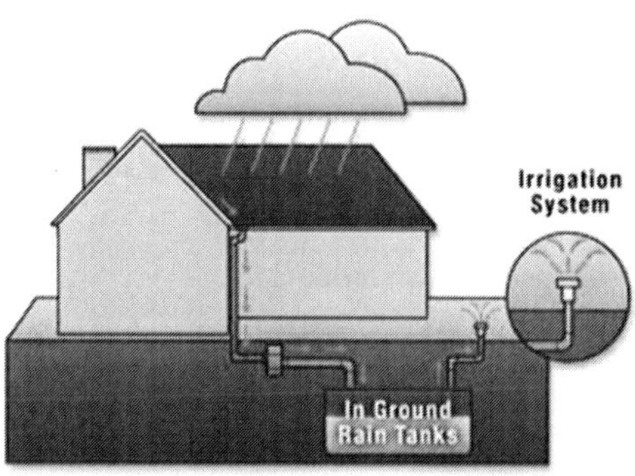

Rainwater Harvesting

What do you need for a water harvesting system is the rain, and a place to collect it! Typically, rainfall is collected on rooftops and other surfaces, and the water is carried down to where it can be stored and used in off rainy season. You can direct water run-off from this surface to plants, trees or lawns or even to the aquifer.

Main benefits of rainwater harvesting are as follows:

- Increases water availability.
- Checks the declining water table.
- Raise the quality of groundwater.
- Prevents soil erosion and flooding especially in urban areas.

Rainwater harvesting: a success story

Cherrapunji is famous because it receives the largest volume of rainfall in the world. It still does but ironically, experiences acute water shortages. This is mainly the result of enormous deforestation and because of the lack of proper methods of conserving rainwater. There has been extensive erosion of soil and often, despite the heavy rainfall and its location in the green hills of Meghalaya, one can see stretches of hillside are mostly devoid of trees and greenery. People have to walk long distances to collect water.

Rainwater Harvesting

In the River surrounding area, Ruparel in Rajasthan, the story is different. This is an example of proper water conservation. This area does not receive even half the rainfall received by Cherrapunji, but proper management and conservation have meant that more water is available than in Cherrapunji in off season.

In this area, the water level in the river began to decline due to the extensive deforestation and agricultural activities along the banks and, by the 1980s, a drought-like situation started spreading. Under the guidance of some NGOs, the women living in the area were encouraged to take the initiative in building johads, i.e., round ponds, and dams to hold back rainwater. Gradually, water began coming back due to following the proper methods of conserving and harvesting rainwater. The revival of the river has transformed the ecology of this area of the place and the lives of the people living along its banks. Their relationship of man with their natural environment has been strengthened. It has proved that humankind is not the master of the environment, but a part of it. If human beings put in an effort, the damage caused by us can be undone.

CASE STUDY

Pani Panchayat, Pune District, Maharashtra

Mahue village, in Pune District of Maharashtra, is situated in a drought-prone area. The people were not able to grow a good crop in most years; clean drinking water was also scarce. A man named Vilasrao Salunkhe initiated a movement, known as *PaniPanchayat,* to conserve water in this drought-prone area. Watershed development was initiated on a barren and uncultivated piece of land belonging to a temple. Soil conservation and water harvesting is brought about through a holistic micro-watershed management programme, gradually led irrigation, 2.4 ha were afforested and 4 ha were converted into percolation tanks. Wells and field bunds were created. While 200 quintals of grains were produced from 24 acres of Salunkhe's land, 40 acres in the same area yielded only 10 quintals. This has however, made other villagers follow suit, and the area rapidly turned green and productive.

Agriculture

Water conservation in the agricultural sector is essential since water is essential for the growth of plants and crops. A depleting water-table and increase in salinity due to overuse of chemical fertilisers and pesticides has made matters serious. However, various methods of water harvesting and water recharging have been and are being applied all over the world to tackle this water problem. In areas where rainfall is low and water is scarce, the local people have used simple traditional techniques that are quite suited to their regions and reduce the demand for water. In India's arid and semi-arid areas, the 'tank' system is traditionally used and also the backbone of agricultural production. Tanks are constructed either by bunding or by excavating the ground and collecting rainwater.

Rajasthan is located in the Great Indian Desert and receives very less rainfall, but people have adapted to the harsh conditions by collecting rainfalls during rainy seasons. Large bunds to create reservoirs are known as khadin, dams are called johads, tanks, and other methods were applied to check water flow and accumulate run-off. After the monsoon season, water from these structures was used to cultivate agriculture crops. Similar systems were developed in many other parts of the country. These are known by various local names as *jaltalais* in Uttar Pradesh, the *haveli* system in Madhya Pradesh, *ahar* in Bihar, and so on.

1. Do not overwater. Provide plants water only they need.
2. Ensure that irrigation equipment is installed properly and functioning well.
3. Use water-conserving devices like, rain a shut-off, soil moisture sensors and check valves.
4. Select timers with 'cycle and soak' capabilities. A first shorter cycle allows water to break through any crusty, dry layer; allowing a later, longer cycle to soak into the soil, reducing runoff.

Reducing water demand

However, the simple techniques adopted can be useful to reduce the demand for water. The underlying principle is that only a little part of the rainfall or irrigation water is taken up by plants and the rest percolates into the deep groundwater or lost by evaporation from the surface. Therefore, by improving the efficiency of water use and by reducing its loss due to evaporation, we can reduce water demand. There are various methods to reduce such losses and to improve soil moisture. Some of them are listed as, Mulching, i.e., the application of organic or inorganic material such as plant debris, compost, etc., slows down the surface run-off, improves the soil moisture and reduces evaporation loss and improves soil fertility. Soil covered by crops, slows down run-off and minimizes evaporation loss. Hence, fields should not be left out bare for long periods of time.

Ploughing helps to move soil around and as a consequence it retains more water thereby reducing evaporation. Shelter belts of trees and bushes along the edge of agricultural fields slow down the wind speed and reduce evaporation and erosion of soil. Plantation of trees, grass, and bushes breaks the force of rain and helps rainwater penetrate the soil. Fog and dew contain substantial amounts of water that can be used directly by adapted plant species. Artificial surfaces such as netting-surfaced traps or polyethylene sheets can be exposed to fog and dew. The resulting stored water can be further used for crops. Contour farming is adopted in hilly areas and in lowland areas for paddy fields. Farmers recognize the efficiency of contour-based systems for conserving soil and water.

Salt-resistant varieties of crops have also been developed recently. As these grow in saline areas, overall agricultural productivity is increased without making additional demands on freshwater sources. Thus, this is a good water conservation strategy to transfer water from surplus areas to deficit areas by inter-linking water systems through canals, etc. Desalination technologies like, distillation, electro-dialysis and reverse osmosis are also available. Use of efficient watering system like, drip irrigation and sprinklers methods will reduce the water consumption by plants.

One of the major important steps in the direction of finding solutions to issues of water and environmental conservation is to change people's attitudes and habits which include each one of us.

Conserve water because it is the right thing to do. We can follow some of the simple things that have been listed below and contribute to conservation of water. Try to do one thing each day that will result in saving water. Don't worry if the savings are minimal because every drop count! And by doing this you can make a difference. Remember to use only the amount you actually need. Form a group of water-conscious people and encourage your friends and neighbours to be part of this group.

Promote water conservation in community newsletters and on bulletin boards. Encourage your friends, neighbours and co-workers to also contribute. Encourage your family to keep looking for new ways to conserve water in and around your home. Make sure that your home is leak-free. Many homes have leaking pipes that go unnoticed. Do not leave the tap running while you are brushing your teeth or soaping your face. See that there are no leaks in the toilet tank. You can check this by adding colour to the tank. If there is a leak, colour will appear in the toilet bowl within 30 minutes. (Flush as soon as the test is done, since food colouring may stain the tank.). Avoid flushing the toilet unnecessarily. Put a brick or any other device that occupies space to cut down on the amount of water needed for each flush. When washing the car, use water from a bucket and not a hosepipe. Do not throw away water that has been used for washing vegetables, rice or dals use it to water plants or to clean the floors, etc. You can store water in a variety of ways. A simple method is to place a drum on a raised platform directly under the rainwater collection source. You can also collect water in a bucket during the rainy season.

1. Repair dripping fixtures, as a one drop per second leak will amount to over 2500 gallons of water waste per year.
2. Use faucet aerators to reduce water use in sinks and lavatories.
3. Take short, 5-minute showers. Use low-flow showerhead and turn off the water while lathering.
4. While shaving, fill the lavatory with warm water, instead of using a running faucet.
5. When brushing your teeth, turn off the water until finished brushing.
6. While washing vegetables, fill a bowl instead of rinsing with running water. Use the used water to your house plants.
7. Change old toilets with other High Efficiency Toilet (HET) using not more than 1.3 gallons per flush.
8. Make sure that all exposed to hot water pipes are insulated.
9. Use hot water recirculation pump to avoid sending cold water down the drain while waiting for hot water.

It is noticeable that conservation of potable water costs less than treating non-potable water and is more sustainable. Water conservation strategies are relatively easy to adopt. However, it is essential to encourage customers to conserve water through public education and incentives for equipment upgrades. Water-efficient technologies and lifestyle modifications can work together to drastically reduce water use.

Conservation of water offers a number of benefits to you, society, and the natural environment:

- Helps you reduce your water bill.
- It helps to save energy associated with delivering water from distant reservoirs and treating it to use for drinking water.
- Reduced energy consumption translates into reduced air pollution from power plants.

- It reduces imported water from the Sierras, the Delta, underground aquifers, and other water sources. This however, conserves water for fisheries, wildlife, agriculture, and essential human needs and reduces the need for extra water storage.
- Conservation of water in the landscape reduces runoff into streams from landscaped areas, which improves watershed water quality.

Soil Conservation

Soil in its broadest sense is an integral part of our human habitat. We totally depend on it for almost everything. However, our dependence on the soil is not reflected in the way we organise or manage it. Inadvertently, it is all too easy to focus on one thing that the soil is doing and then to ignore others, especially those things which are for long term. In order to achieve a proper land use, it is necessary for people to have a better, proper understanding of what is going on in the soil.

Under the natural conditions, various environmental factors evolve which vary according to the available variety of plants and animals and the existing soil, climate and topographic conditions. These environments exist in a state of dynamic equilibrium, a state where they are generally able to adjust and recover after some uncommon events like, the outbreak of a disease, a fire, or a drought. Wherever humans have settled and cultivated and grazed the land with their domesticated animals, these conditions have been upset and changed. However, at some places, and over time, new forms of land use patterns have evolved which are in harmony with the soil, climate, and topography and a new, productive and stable environment has been established. Unfortunately, this has not always been the case and over large areas of the world's surface, land use systems are to be found which are not in balance and wherever this is the case, various forms of land degradation are taking place.

Soil conservation is a process of solving the problems of land degradation, particularly accelerated erosion of soil. Accelerated erosion of soil is a result of the operation of the physical forces of

Soil Conservation

wind and water on soil, which has become heavily vulnerable generally because of human interference with the natural environment. For this reason, erosion of soil can be viewed as a symptom of bad land use and management.

Land degradation is not a new problem. In fact, erosion of soil, soil salinity and other related forms of land degradation have been with us from the time when humans first started domesticated animals, settled, and started to raise crops, at least 7000 years ago. At times, the problem of land degradation has become very severe that it has contributed to, if not caused, the decline of great civilisations in such places such as China, Mesopotamia, Egypt, North Africa, and Greece.

Confronted with the problem of land degradation, over the centuries, farmers have developed indigenous strategies and systems of land use and management to preserve, protect and rehabilitate their lands. Many of these have been quite effective and the remains of some of them can still be seen in old terracing systems in various countries like, Yemen, China, and Peru, as well as in farming systems such as shifting cultivation which is still practiced in parts of the tropics.

Great interest has been shown in these traditional soil-conservation systems in recent years and a number of studies have been conducted to find out more about them and if they can be adapted to present-day conditions.

Soil conservation is the method of management strategies for the prevention of soil erosion from the Earth's surface by overuse, acidification, salination or other chemical soil contamination. It is also a component of environmental soil science. Soil conservation is, however, a fundamental matter of determining a right form of land use and management. A correct form of land use and management thus provides a higher level or a different form of productivity available in the natural state. Thus, this new form of productivity must be capable of being sustained indefinitely.

Soil Degradation

Soil conservation can be defined as the combination of the appropriate land use and management practices that promotes the productive and sustainable use of soils and, in the process, minimizes soil erosion, desertification and other forms of land degradation.

Soil conservation is a process of maintaining good health of soil by various practices. The aim of soil conservation is to prevent erosion of soil and also to prevent soil contamination from chemicals. There are numerous measures that are used to maintain good soil health, and prevent from the above harms to soil. There are various ways to conserve soil which are suited to those areas where farming is done according to the need of soil. Here are some soil conservation practices as:

Planting Vegetation

It is one of the most suitable and cost saving strategy. This measure is one of the various soil conservation techniques used by farmers. By planting trees, grass, plants, erosion of soil can be greatly prevented. Plants help to stabilise the soil properties and trees act as a wind barrier to prevent soil from being eroded. This is also one among various strategies used for soil conservation in urban areas, where one can plant trees and plants in the landscape areas of the residential places. The best practiced choices for the vegetation are herbs, small trees, plants with wild flowers, and creepers which provide cover for ground.

To understand this strategy, it is important to recognize the forces of wind and rain can exerted on the bare soil. For example, the energy dissipated by a 50 mm rain storm is theoretically capable enough of lifting 18 cm of soils to 1 meter into the air. If the raindrops are large in size, they fragment soil clods and disperse them in all directions. If there is a cover of vegetation on the earth surface, living or dead, the soil is protected as the energy of the falling raindrops is dissipated when they strike the vegetation. Research into this subject shows that the vegetation does provide a complete cover to be effective if, about 40% of the soil's surface is protected by low-level vegetation, i.e., not more than 1 meter above the surface, and evenly distributed cover erosion can be reduced by as much as 90%.

Not only this, but a cover of vegetation on the ground slows down the movement of water across the surface and allows it to sink into the soil, becoming available to the roots of plants or percolating down to the water table. Also, if vegetation can be retained, and allowed to break down and become part of the soil, the physical and chemical properties of the soil are improved. This, in turn, makes the soil less susceptible to erosion and more conducive to plant growth.

A method called '*agroforestry*' has been widely promoted and accepted in the tropics in recent years. In this practice, trees and crops are grown together in the same field. The trees are often grown in narrow strips, often on the contour, and are generally cut at different times so that they do not provide shade that would affect the growing field crops. The trees may be either fruit trees or trees which have the ability to trap nitrogen from the atmosphere and return it to the soil where it can be used by other plants.

Trees are used in many ways to protect the soil. They are particularly effective as wind breakers and are frequently used to control erosion and reclaim badly degraded land. However, trees are seldom very effective on their own as soil cover needs to be no more than about 1 meter above the surface of the soil to prevent water erosion. A good ground cover of grasses, shrubs, and/or leaf litter is needed if the trees are to effectively control water erosion.

Contour Plowing

The simplest method of mechanical erosion control is contours plowing. This method is consisted of cultivation of the land on or close to the contour instead of up and down the slope round the field. When this is done, each furrow acts as a small dam, catching water as it runs down the hill and encouraging it to soak into the soil. This simple conservation measure may be enough by itself to prevent the runoff of water and erosion where slopes are gentle and the rainfall intensities are low.

Contour banks have been used successfully to control erosion over large areas of cultivated land, particularly in the USA, Australia, and parts of South America. These often involve complex systems with earthen banks carefully built on grades close to the contour, but with a sufficient slope to allow excess water to gently run away. The excess water is usually diverted to artificial waterways down which the water can safely run until it reaches a natural stream or watercourse. These systems have proved to be very effective on cultivated land where the farms and the fields are large. However, it is a system that has failed to be accepted by farmers in Africa and Asia where the fields are generally small and fragmented. Under these prevailing conditions, the complex contour systems are too hard to manage as they must cross numerous field boundaries. Also, the banks and waterways take up land and are relatively unproductive-something which is unacceptable to small farmers who are, not willing to lose the use of any part of their small plots.

Contour farming is used by farmers in which they plow across a slope and follow the elevation of contour lines. This method prevents water run-off, and thus prevents erosion of soil by allowing water to slowly penetrate the soil.

Maintaining the Soil pH

The measurement of soil's acidity or alkalinity is done by measuring pH level of the soils. Soil gets polluted due to the addition of basic or acidic pollutants which can be checked by maintaining the desirable level of pH of soil.

Soil Organisms

In the absence of the activities performed by soil organisms, the organic material required by vegetation will litter and would not be available for growth. Using beneficial soil organisms like earthworms, helps in aeration of soil and makes the macro-nutrients available for the plants. Thus, the soil becomes more fertile and porous.

Crop Rotation Practice

Crop rotation is the soil conservation method where a series of different crops are planted one after the other in the same soil area. This method is used greatly in organic farming. It is done to prevent the accumulation of pathogens, which occur if the same plants are grown in the soil, and also depletion of nutrients.

Watering the Soil

We water plants and trees, but it is equally essential to provide water to soil to maintain its health. Soil erosion occurs if the soil is being eroded by wind. By watering and settling the soil, one can prevent erosion of soil from the blowing away of soil by wind. One of the effective soil conservation methods in India is the drip irrigation system which provides water to the soil without the water running-off.

Salinity Management

Excessive collection of salts in the soil has harmful effects on the metabolism of plants. Salinity can lead to death of the vegetation and thus cause soil erosion, which is why salinity management is important.

Terracing

Terracing is one of the best soil conservation methods, where cultivation is done on a terrace. In terracing, farming is done on a unique step like structure and the possibility of water running off is lowered down.

Bordering from Indigenous Crops

It is preferable to native plants, but when native plants are not planted then bordering the crops with indigenous crops is necessary. This helps to prevent soil erosion, and this measure is greatly opted in poor rural areas.

No-tilling Farming Method

The soil plowed process for farming is called tilling, wherein the fertilisers are mixed and the rows for plantation are created. However, this method leads to death of beneficial soil microorganisms, loss of organic matter and compaction of soil and hence due to these side effects, the no-tilling strategy is used to conserve soil health.

These were the major 10 ways to conserve and preserve soil which are used across the world. Soil is a precious constituent, and is developed through a long process of weathering and disintegration of weathering rocks which turn into sand or clay. The clay like fertile soil provides home to organisms like earthworms, beetles, ants other micro-organisms which live in it. Soil provides support to plants and trees. The plants and trees provide home to birds and animals. The crops growing on the soil provide us food, shelter and clothes. Thus, soil defines the quality of human life around it that is why it is important to use these methods. Branches of environmental science like Earth science are constantly trying to find new methods, for maintaining the ecological balance. In different parts of the world, people are studying soil science and coming up with different new beneficial soil conservation techniques.

Treatment of Waste

In various ancient cities, food and other related wastes were simply thrown into the unpaved streets where they accumulate. Around 320 BC in Athens, the first known law to forbid this practice was established, and a system of waste removal began to evolve in various eastern Mediterranean cities. The initial disposal practices were very crude and were often just open pits outside the city wells. As the population was increased over time, efforts were made to transport the wastes out away from the cities, thus creating city dumps. Until recently, the disposal of urban solid waste did not attract much public attention. The favoured means of urban waste disposal was to dump solid wastes outside the city or village limits, and occasionally burn or compact them. Around the most towns and cities in India, the approaching roads are littered with multicoloured plastic bags and other useless garbage.

Waste is also, however, burnt to reduce its volume. Modern practices of disposal like, incineration and the development of sanitary landfills, etc., are now attempting to solve these problems. The lack of space for dumping solid waste has become a serious problem in many cities and towns all over the world. Today, from an environment of health perspective, dumping and burning wastes is not an acceptable practice. The disposal of solid waste should be the part of an integrated waste management plan.

Solid wastes are grouped or classified in various different ways. These different classifications are essential to address the growing challenges of solid waste management in an effective manner. The term municipal solid waste is generally used to describe most of the non-hazardous solid waste from a city, town or village that requires routine collection and transport to a processing or disposal site. Sources of MSW include private homes, commercial establishments and institutions as well as industrial facilities. However, Municipal Solid Waste does not include waste from industrial processes, construction and demolition debris, sewage sludge, mining wastes or agricultural wastes.

Municipal solid waste contains varieties of materials, food waste, like vegetable and meat material, leftover food, eggshells etc., which is classified as wet garbage and paper, plastic, tetra packs, plastic cans, newspaper, glass bottles, cardboard boxes, aluminum foil, metal items, wood pieces, etc., which is classified as dry garbage.

Source reduction is one of the principal ways to reduce waste. This can be done by using less material when making a product, reducing products on site, designing products or packaging to reduce their quantity. On an individual basis, we can reduce the use of unnecessary items while shopping and buy items with minimal packaging, avoid buying disposable items and also avoid use for plastic carry bags.

Recycling is the reusing some components of the solid waste that may have some economic value. Recycling has readily visible benefits like conserving resources, reducing energy used during manufacturing, and lessening pollution levels. Some materials, like, aluminum and steel can be recycled various times. Metal, paper, glass and plastics are recyclable. Mining of new aluminium is expensive and, hence, recycled aluminium has a sound market and plays an important role in the aluminium industry. Paper recycling can also help preserve forests, as it takes about 17 trees to make one tonne of paper. Crushed glasses (culled) reduce the energy required to manufacture new glass by 50%. Culled lowers the temperature requirement of glassmaking process thus conserving energy and reducing air pollution.

Disposal of solid waste is done most commonly through a sanitary landfill or through incineration. A modern sanitary landfill is a depression in an impermeable soil layer that is lined with an impermeable membrane. The three key characteristics of a municipal sanitary landfill that distinguish it from an open dump are:

- Solid waste is placed carefully in selected and prepared landfill site.
- The waste material is spread out and compacted with appropriate heavy machinery.
- Each day, the solid waste is covered with a layer of compacted soil.

The older landfills are generally associated with groundwater pollution. Pollutants seeping out from the bottom of a sanitary landfill frequently percolate down to the groundwater aquifer, no matter how thick the underlying soil layer. Today, due to the action of microorganisms, it is necessary to have a suitable bottom-liner and leach ate-collected systems along with the installation of monitoring systems. At first the waste decomposes aerobically until the oxygen that was present in the freshly-placed fill is used up by the aerobic microorganisms. Then the anaerobes take over, releasing methane gas which is poisonous and highly explosive when mixed with air in concentrations between 5 and 15%. The movement of the gas can be controlled by providing impermeable barriers in the landfill. A venting system is developed to collect the blocked gas and vent it to the surface, where it can be safely diluted and dispersed into the atmosphere, is thus a necessary component of the design of sanitary landfills.

Incineration is the process of burning municipal solid waste in a properly-designed furnace under suitable temperature and operating conditions. Incineration is a chemical process in which the combustible portion of the waste is combined with oxygen forming carbon dioxide and water, which are released into atmosphere.

Ecosystem approach is related with the treatment of environmental pollution and resource management as well as environmental protection that aim to consider the complex and intricate interrelationships of an entire ecosystem in decision-making rather than simply responding to specific problem and challenges. Ideally the decision-making processes under such an approach would be a collaborative approach to planning and decision-making that involves a broad range of stakeholders across all relevant governmental departments, and representatives of various industries, environmental groups and concerned community. This approach promotes and supports a better exchange of valuable information, development of conflict-resolution strategies and improved regional conservation.

Environmental pollution is thus inevitable. Generation of waste streams occur from anything we produce and consume. Pollution, however, directly impacts the quality of the receiving medium, i.e. air, water, soil and when this impaired medium acts upon a receptor like, a living organism, also impacts the receptor. In general, the impacts on the receptor are adverse, but not always. Typically, ecosystems have some natural attributes to assimilate pollution. These ecosystems vary considerably with the nature of the pollutant and the ecosystem. Generally, it is cheaper to reduce the emissions of pollution than to mitigate it after generation or to treat. Pollution may differentially impact the poor, women or children, or developing regions, which may also have relatively low contributions in pollutions, and accordingly the costs and benefits of abatement may have important implications for equity.

(i) Air Pollution

Air pollution has the direct adverse impacts on human health, as well as on the health of other living organisms, man-made heritage, and life-support systems, such as global climate. However, depending upon the lifetime of the pollutants, the source of location, and the prevailing atmosphere, the receptors may be located at homestead, local, regional, national or global levels, at time of intervals from near instantaneous to several decades.

The prime causes of air pollution are the emissions from the use of fossil energy like, coal and petroleum, and other industrial processes, and some consumption activities. The deeper causes arise in a multiplicity of policy, and institutional factors, including regulatory shortcoming, in particular, inefficient pricing of fossil fuel-based energy. Indoor air pollution as a special case arises from the low societal status of women, leading to continued use of polluting inefficient biomass stoves, besides pricing policies for agricultural chemicals which lead to substitution of biomass-based fertiliser by chemicals. The biomass is then, being used inefficiently as a source of fuel. These deepening causes need to be addressed through proper policies and programmes for redressing women's status, and dialogue aimed at consideration of the environmental impacts of pricing policies for agricultural chemicals.

In addition, the following specific actions need to be taken:

(a) Accelerate the programmes on national level for the dissemination of improved fuel wood stoves, and solar cookers, suited to local cooking practices.

(b) Strengthen the monitoring system and enforcement of emission standards for both point and non-point sources, with participation of the local communities in monitoring.

(c) Prepare and implement action plans for major urban areas to address air pollution for both point and non-point sources, relying on a judicious combination of fiats and incentive-based instruments.

(d) Carve out a national strategy for urban transport to ensure proper investment, public and private, in low-pollution mass transport systems.

(e) Promote reclamation of wastelands by energy plantations through multi-stakeholder partnerships by involving the land-owning agencies, investors and local communities.

(ii) Water Pollution

In the above study, we have discussed the direct and indirect causes of pollution of surface water sources, groundwater, and coastal areas. The following are some further elements of an action plan:

(a) Develop and implement the plan on a primary pilot scale, public-private partnership models for setting up and operating effluent and sewage treatment plants. Once these models are validated, it progressively uses public resources, including external assistance, to catalyze such partnerships. Enhance the capabilities of municipalities for recovery of user charges for water and sewage systems.

(b) Enhance reuse of treated sewage and industrial wastewater before final discharge to water bodies.

(c) Increase the capacities for spatial planning among the various States and Local Governments, with proper participation by local communities to ensure clustering of polluting industries to facilitate setting up of common effluent treatment plants to be operated on cost recovery basis.

(d) Promote research and development in development of low cost technologies for sewage treatment at various scales, in particular, the replication of the East Kolkata wetlands model for sewage treatment to yield multiple benefits.

(e) Take explicit account of groundwater pollution in pricing policies of agricultural inputs, especially pesticides, and dissemination of agronomy practices involving their use.

(f) Develop a plan for strengthening regulation, and checking the impacts, of ship-breaking activities on coastal and near marine resources.

(iii) Soil Pollution

Similarly, the immediate and deeper causes of soil pollution have been considered above. The following are elements of an action plan:

(a) Develop and implement desirable models of public-private partnerships for setting up and operating secure landfills and incinerators for toxic and hazardous waste, both industrial and biomedical, on payment by users, taking the proper concerns of local communities into account. The concerned local communities and State Governments must have clear entitlements to specified benefits from hosting such sites, if access is given to non-local users.

(b) Develop and implement programmes for clean-up of pre-existing toxic and hazardous waste dumps, in industrial areas, and reclamation of such lands for future, sustainable use.

(c) Strengthen the capabilities of local bodies for segregation, recycling and reuse of urban solid wastes, and setting up and operating sanitary landfills, in particular through competitive outsourcing of solid waste management services.

(d) Give validation to, and strengthen the informal sector systems of collection and recycling of various materials and enhance their access to institutional finance and relevant technologies.

(e) Promote practice of organic farming for traditional crop varieties through research in and dissemination of techniques for reclamation of land with prior exposure to agricultural chemicals, provide marketing of organic produce in India and abroad, including by development of transparent, voluntary, science-based labelling schemes.

(f) Develop and implement strategies for recycle, reuse, and final environmentally benign disposal of plastics wastes, including through promotion of relevant technologies, and use of incentive-based instruments.

(iv) Noise Pollution

Persistent exposure to increasing noise levels has been established to result in an adverse health impact. While in many cases, the identification of a particular sound as "noise" is unambiguous, in the case of others, such as "music" or "chanting" or "fireworks display", it is inherently subjective. In all such instances, the well-being of society would require that exposure levels to third parties be maintained below levels at which significant adverse health impacts may occur.

At the same time, it needs to be understood that certain environments in which people choose to live and work necessarily involve a certain level of noise. The following would comprise elements of an Action Plan on abatement of noise pollution:

(a) Make proper distinctions between various environments in terms of setting ambient noise standards, like, rural versus urban; educational and medical establishments versus other areas; nighttime versus daytime in residential areas; areas in the vicinity of road, rail, and airport infrastructure; etc.

(b) Differentiate between noise standards and protection measures in the context of occupational exposure, and environmental exposure to third parties.

(c) Formulate proper noise emissions norms for loudspeaker, automobile horns, fireworks ratings, and appropriate ways to ensure that exposure levels to third parties who are not participants in the activity do not exceed prescribed ambient standards.

(d) Encourage dialogue and talk between State/Local Authorities and religious/community representatives for the adoption of enforceable specific durations, timings, and use of loud-speakers/fireworks, etc. in case temporary exceedance of prescribed ambient noise standards for observance of traditional religious/cultural/social events cannot be avoided.

The discussion concerned with environmental protection often focuses on the role of government, legislation and law enforcement. However, in its broadest sense, environmental protection may be seen as the responsibility of all people and not simply that of government. However, the decisions that impact the environment will ideally involve a broad range of stakeholders like, industry, indigenous groups, environmental groups and community representatives. Gradually, decision-making processes of the environments are evolving to reflect this broad base of stakeholders and are becoming more collaborative in many countries.

Many constitutions recognize fundamental right to environmental protection, and many international treaties acknowledge the right to live in a healthy natural environment. Also, many countries have organisations and agencies devoted to environmental protection.

Many of the earth's resources are critically vulnerable because they are affected by human impacts across various countries. As a result, to this, various attempts are made by countries to develop agreements that are signed by multiple governments to prevent damage or manage the impacts of human activity on natural resources. This can include pacts and agreements that impact factors such as climate, oceans, rivers and air pollution. These international environmental agreements are sometimes legally binding documents that have legal implications when they are not followed and, at other times, are more agreements in principle or are for use as codes of conduct.

The challenges of environmental protection are intrinsically connected with the state of environment resource such as land, air and flora and fauna. Environmental planning involves the implementation of environmental protection and mitigation measures and monitoring for significant environmental impacts. Environmental protection measures are taken to:

(i) mitigate environmental impacts,

(ii) provide in-kind compensation for lost environmental resources,

(iii) enhance environmental resources.

In order to reduce and eliminate the adverse impacts, these measures are to be undertaken to ensure compliance with environmental regulations. However, the basic implementation arrangements must be presented, taking proper account of the local conditions. Responsibilities for mitigation and monitoring shall be defined along with arrangements for the flow of information, and for coordination between concerned agencies responsible for mitigation of environmental problems. Environment planning should specify which agency is responsible for undertaking the mitigating and monitoring measures, e.g., for enforcement of remedial actions, monitoring, training, and financing.

With the increasing population and demand of the available natural resources it is pertinent to conserve natural resources for the further use in the future. For this sustainable development is a vital phenomenon which aims at utilising the natural resources without compromising the future quality of the same for human need. Environmental pollution has created an atmosphere where there is difficult have good quality of life with dignity. Hence, there is need to carve out an environmental planning so that there is a proper way of development of our common environment for the welfare of the society as a whole.

The development and implementation and effective national policies and laws relating to environment protection will depend on decision-makers having access to relevant and definitive information from different stakeholders. Any strategic approach should, therefore, undertake and support timely, participatory expertise, knowledge data and indicators.

Chapter - 5

Environmental Protection and Promotion

Environmental protection is a method and process of protecting the natural environment on individual, organisational or governmental levels for the benefit of the natural environment and humans. With the increasing pressures of population and technology, the biophysical environment is being degraded, sometimes permanently. This has been recognised, and governments have begun placing restraints on activities that cause environmental degradation. Since 1960, activities of environmental movements have created awareness of the various environmental issues. There is no agreement on the extent of the environmental impact of human activity, and protection measures are occasionally criticized.

In the recent decades there has emerged a consciousness about the protection and conservation of environment world-wide. Academic institutions now offer courses, such as environmental studies, environmental management and environmental engineering, that teach the history and methods of environment protection. Environmental protection is needed due to various human activities. Waste production, air pollution, and loss of biodiversity resulting from the introduction of invasive species and species extinction are some of the issues related to environmental protection.

Environmental protection is directly influenced by three interwoven factors like, environmental legislation, ethics and education. Each of these factors plays its part in affecting national level environmental decisions and personal level environmental values and behaviours. For environmental protection to become a reality, it is essential for societies to develop each of these areas that, together, will inform and drive environmental decisions.

The quality of environment in India has deteriorated severely during past two decades. This is mainly because of the gap between the intent of the policy and the actual achievement. India's environmental problems are mainly because of its high population growth and limited available natural resources. Thus, protection of the environment poses a fundamental challenge to the nation's desire to industrialise faster. Various efforts are being made to control India's environmental problems.

The government of India has recognised the need for planned land and water resource management and the protection of environmental resources is included in the constitution since 1976. The constitutional 42th amendment act of 1977 obligates the Government to protect and improve the quality of environment for the welfare of society as a whole. It also makes environmental protection an obligation of the state and individual citizen and reads, "The state shall Endeavour to protect and improve the environment and to safeguard forests and wildlife of the country." Article 51-A (9) states, "It shall be duty of every citizen of India to protect and improve the natural environment including forests, lakes, rivers, wildlife and to have compassion for living creatures."

India's first national law of environment was the Insecticidal Act enacted in 1968 for regulating the import, manufacture, sale, transport, distribution and use of insecticides in order to reduce risk to human beings or animals.

The year 1972 was proved to be a land mark in the history of Indian environmental management. However, India attempted the first national efforts to address environmental protection through the formulation of National Committee on Environmental Planning and Co-ordination (NCEPC). The NCEPC was established in 1972 to prepare a report on the state of environment in India for the Human Environment Conference at Stockholm. In June 1972 it was established to promote greater co-ordination and integration in environmental programmes and policies.

In the same year (1972) the wildlife protection act was enacted to provide for the protection of wild animals and birds. The act provided the constituent of a Wildlife Advisory Board for each state, regulation of the hunting of wild animals and birds, and specified procedures for declaring areas are as Sanctuaries and National Parks. It has also provided for regulation of possession, acquisition and trade in wild animals and animal products. However, implementation of the act was far from being satisfactory. It failed to prevent hunting of rare animals and trade in the wildlife products.

The first national law for pollution control was enacted in 1974. The water (Prevention and Control of Pollution) Act of 1974 thus marked an important milestone in environmental legislation in India. The act provides for the establishment of pollution control boards at the centre and states for the purpose of prevention, abatement and control of water pollution.

National Policy on Environment

A diverse and fast-growing developing society such as ours provides various challenges in the economic, social, political, cultural, and environmental arenas. All of these coalesce in the dominant imperative of alleviation of mass poverty, reckoned in the multiple dimensions of food security, healthcare facility, education, empowerment of the disadvantaged and elimination of gender disparities. The National Environment Policy 2006 aims to extend the coverage, and fill in gaps that still exist, in the light of present knowledge and accumulated experience. It does not displace, but builds on the earlier policies.

However, across the political spectrum of the country there has been recognition of the major role natural resources play in providing livelihoods and securing life support ecological services. In this perspective, a need for a holistic approach and proper policy statement has been evident for some time in order to infuse a common approach to the various sectoral and cross-sectoral, including fiscal, approaches to environmental management. As our development challenges have evolved and our understanding of the centrality of environmental concerns in development has sharpened, there is also a dire need to review the earlier objectives, policy instruments, and strategies.

This requires an evolving and generous policy framework with a built-in system for monitoring and review, and where necessary, revision. Concerns for sustainable development in the sense of enhancement of human welfare, broadly conceived, are a recurring theme in India's development philosophy. The present-day unanimous consensus reflects three foundational aspirations: First, human beings should be able to enjoy a decent quality of life; second, that humanity should become capable enough to respect the finiteness of the biosphere; and third, that neither the aspiration for the good life, nor the recognition of biophysical limits should preclude the search for greater justice in the world.

For this to occur there is a need for balanced growth between economic, social and environmental needs of the country. India also plays significant role in various significant international initiatives concerned with the natural environment. It is a party to the key multilateral agreements, and recognizes the interdependencies among, and trans-boundary character of, several environmental problems.

The National Environment Policy is also focussed to be a statement of India's commitment to making a positive contribution to international efforts.

This National Environment Policy is a response to Indian governments' commitment to a clean environment, mandated in the Indian Constitution under the Articles 48 A and 51 A (g), strengthened by judicial interpretation of Article 21. It is however, recognised that maintaining a healthy environment is not the state's responsibility alone, but also that of every citizen. A spirit of partnership should thus be realised throughout the spectrum of environmental management in the country. While the state must galvanise its efforts, there should also be recognition by each individual - natural or institutional, of its responsibility towards maintaining and enhancing the quality of the environment.

The National Environment Policy has been centered and motivated by the above considerations and is mainly intended to mainstream environmental concerns in all development activities. It briefly, however, describes the key environmental challenges presently and prospectively facing by India. The objectives of environment policy and normative principles underlying policy action are strategic themes for intervention, broad indications of the legislative and institutional development, needed to accomplish the strategic themes, and mechanisms for implementation and review. It has been prepared through a process of comprehensive and extensive consultation with experts, as well as diverse stakeholders, and this process is also documented.

The National Environment Policy is mainly intended to be a guide to action: in regulatory reform, programmes and projects for natural environmental conservation and review and enactment of appropriate legislation by agencies of the Central, State and Local Governments. The policy also seeks to stimulate partnerships of different stakeholders like, public agencies, local communities, academic and scientific institutions, the investment community, and international development partners, in harnessing their respective natural resources and strengths for environmental management. The principal theme of this policy is that while conservation of environmental natural resources it is necessary to secure livelihoods and well-being of all. However, the most secure basis for environmental conservation is to ensure that people dependent on particular natural resources obtain better livelihoods from the fact of conservation, than from degradation of the resources.

NATIONAL ENVIRONMENT POLICY 2004

Forestland

The National environmental policy 2004 is highly centered and intended to be a guide to action: in regulatory reform, programmes and projects for environmental conservation; and review and enactment of legislation, by agencies of the Central, State, and Local Governments. It also seeks to stimulate partnerships of different stakeholders, i.e. public agencies, local communities, the investment community, and international development partners, in harnessing their respective resources and strengths for environmental management. On the whole, it is expected to do better than fiscal neutrality, and likely raise substantial resources from outside the fiscal regime to realise its objectives.

The Objectives of NEP 2004

The principal objectives of this policy are enumerated below. These objectives relate to current perceptions of key environmental challenges. They may, accordingly, evolve over time:

- *Conservation of Critical Environmental Resources:* To protect and conserve critical ecological systems and resources, and invaluable natural and man-made heritage which are essential for life support, livelihoods, economic growth, and a broad conception of human well-being.
- *Intra-generational Equity and Livelihood Security for the Poor:* To ensure suitable and equitable access to environmental resources and quality for all sections of society and in particular, to ensure that poor communities, which are mostly dependent on environmental resources for their livelihoods, are assured to secure access to these resources.
- *Inter-generational Equity:* To ensure judicious use of environmental resources to meet the needs and aspirations of present and future generations.
- *Integration of Environmental Concerns in Economic and Social Development:* To integrate environmental concerns into policies, plans, programmes, and projects for economic and social development.
- *Efficiency in Environmental Resource Use:* To ensure efficient use of environmental resources in the sense of reduction in their use per unit of economic output, to minimize adverse environmental impacts.
- *Environmental Governance:* Includes the principles of good governance like, transparency, rationality, accountability, reduction in time and costs, and participation to the management and regulation of use of environmental resources.
- *Enhancement of Resources for Environmental Conservation:* To ensure greater resource flows, comprising finance, technology, management skills, traditional knowledge, and

social capital, for environmental conservation through mutually beneficial multi stakeholder partnerships between local communities, public agencies, and investors.

Laws on Environmental Protection

In the Indian Constitution, it is clearly mentioned that it is the duty of the state to 'protect and improve the environment and to safeguard the forests and wildlife of the country'. It imposes a duty on every citizen 'to protect and improve the natural environment including forests, lakes, rivers, and wildlife'. Reference to the environment has also been made in the Fundamental Rights and Directive Principles of State Policy. The Department of Environment was established in India in 1980 to ensure a healthy environment for the country. This later became the Ministry of Environment and Forests in 1985. The constitutional provisions are backed by a number of laws- acts, rules, and notifications. The Environment Protection Act 1986 came into force soon after the Bhopal Gas Tragedy and is considered an umbrella legislation as it fills many gaps in the existing laws. Thereafter a large number of laws came into existence as the problems began arising, for example, Handling and Management of Hazardous Waste Rules in 1989.

The Environment (Protection) Act 1986

This Act was formulated in the aftermath of the Bhopal Gas Tragedy in 1984 claiming more than 3000 lives. The Statement of Objects and Reasons of this Act refers to the decisions taken at the Stockholm Conference in June 1972 and expresses concern about the decline in environmental quality, increasing pollution, loss of vegetal cover and biological diversity, excessive concentrations of harmful chemicals in the ambient atmosphere, growing risks of environmental accidents and threats of life system.

According to this Act environment is consists of water, air and land and the interrelationship which exists among and between water, air and land, and human beings, other living creatures, plants, micro-organism and property. This act defines hazardous substance as 'any substance or preparation which, by reasons of its chemical or

Biodiversity

physiochemical properties or handling, is liable to cause harm to human beings, other living creatures, plants, micro-organism, property or the environment'.

This Act gives the following powers to the central government:

- coordination and cooperation of actions of the state governments, officers and other authorities under the Act or any other law which is relatable to the objects of the Act;
- planning and execution of a nation-wide programme for the protection, prevention, control of environmental pollution;
- laying down standards for the quality of environment in its various aspects;
- laying down standards for emission or discharge of environmental pollutants from various sources;
- restriction of areas in which any industry, operations or processes or class of industries, operations or processes shall not be carried out subject to certain safeguards;

- laying down planning and procedures and safeguards for the prevention of accidents which may cause environmental pollution and remedial measures for such accidents;
- examination and review of such manufacturing processes, materials and substances which may cause environmental pollution;
- carrying out and sponsoring investigations and research relating to problems of environmental pollution;
- inspection of any unit, equipment, machinery, manufacturing or other processes, materials or substances and giving, by order, of such directions to such authorities, offers or persons as it may consider to take steps for the prevention, control and abatement of environmental pollution;
- establishment or recognition of environmental laboratories and institutions;
- collection and dissemination of information in respect of matters relating to environmental pollution; and
- preparation of manuals, codes of conducts and guides relating to the prevention, control and abatement of environmental pollution.

The central government may make rules covering the following matters:

(i) The standards of quality of air, water or soil for various areas and purposes;

(ii) The maximum allowable limits of concentration of various environmental pollutants including noise for different areas;

(iii) The procedures and safeguards for the handling of hazardous substances;

(iv) The prohibitions and restrictions on the handling of hazardous substances in various areas;

(v) The prohibitions and restrictions on the location of industries and the carrying on the process and operation in different areas; and

(vi) The procedures and safeguards for the prevention of accidents which may cause environmental pollution.

The central government may constitute an authority or authorities for the purpose of exercising such powers and functions under this Act.

Following is a list of the environmental legislations that have come into effect:

General

The Environment (Protection) Act 1986 authorises the central government to protect and improve environmental quality, control and reduce pollution from all sources, and prohibit or restrict the setting and /or operation of any industrial facility on environmental grounds.

The Environment (Protection) Rules 1986 lay down procedures for setting standards of emission or discharge of environmental pollutants.

The objective of Hazardous Waste (Management and Handling) Rules 1989 is to control the generation, collection, treatment, import, storage, and handling of hazardous waste.

The Manufacture, Storage, and Import of Hazardous Rules 1989 define the terms used in this context, and sets up an authority to inspect, once a year, the industrial activity connected with hazardous chemicals and isolated storage facilities.

1989-The Manufacture, Use, Import, Export, and Storage of hazardous Micro-organisms/ Genetically Engineered Organisms or Cells Rules were introduced with a view to protect the environment, nature, and health, in connection with the application of gene technology and microorganisms.

The Public Liability Insurance Act and Rules and Amendment, 1992 was drawn up to provide for public liability insurance for the purpose of providing immediate relief to the persons affected by accident while handling any hazardous substance.

The National Environmental Tribunal Act 1995 has been created to award compensation for damages to persons, property, and the environment arising from any activity involving hazardous substances.

The National Environment Appellate Authority Act 1997 has been created to hear appeals with respect to restrictions of areas in which classes of industries etc. are carried out or prescribed subject to certain safeguards under the EPA.

The Biomedical Waste (Management and Handling) Rules 1998 is a legal binding on the healthcare institutions to streamline the process of proper handling of hospital waste such as segregation, disposal, collection, and treatment.

The Environment (Siting for Industrial Projects) Rules, 1999 lay down detailed provisions relating to areas to be avoided for siting of industries, precautionary measures to be taken for site selecting as also the aspects of environmental protection which should have been incorporated during the implementation of the industrial development projects.

The Municipal Solid Wastes (Management and Handling) Rules, 2000 apply to every municipal authority responsible for the collection, segregation, storage, transportation, processing, and disposal of municipal solid wastes.

Picture: Wildlife Protection

The Ozone Depleting Substances (Regulation and Control) Rules 2000 have been laid down for the regulation of production and consumption of ozone depleting substances.

The Batteries (Management and Handling) Rules, 2001 rules shall apply to every manufacturer, importer, re-conditioner, assembler, dealer, auctioneer, consumer, and bulk consumer involved in the manufacture, processing, sale, purchase, and use of batteries or components so as to regulate and ensure the environmentally safe disposal of used batteries.

The Noise Pollution (Regulation and Control) (Amendment) Rules 2002 lay down such terms and conditions as are necessary to reduce noise pollution, permit use of loud speakers or public address systems during night hours (between 10:00 p.m. to 12:00 midnight) on or during any cultural or religious festive occasion.

The Biological Diversity Act 2002 is an act to provide for the conservation of biological diversity, sustainable use of its components, and fair and equitable sharing of the benefits arising out of the use of biological resources and knowledge associated with it.

Forest and wildlife

The Indian Forest Act and Amendment, 1984, is one of the many surviving colonial statutes. It was enacted to 'consolidate the law related to forest, the transit of forest produce, and the duty leviable on timber and other forest produce'.

The Wildlife Protection Act, Rules 1973 and Amendment 1991 provides for the protection of birds and animals and for all matters that are connected to it whether it be their habitat or the waterhole or the forests that sustain them.

1980 - The Forest (Conservation) Act and Rules, 1981, provides for the protection of and the conservation of the forests.

Water

The Easement Act 1882 allows private rights to use a resource that is, groundwater, by viewing it as an attachment to the land. It also states that all surface water belongs to the state and is a state property.

The Indian Fisheries Act 1897 establishes two sets of penal offences whereby the government can sue any person who uses dynamite or other explosive substance in any way (whether coastal or inland) with intent to catch or destroy any fish or poisonous fish in order to kill.

The River Boards Act 1956 enables the states to enroll the central government in setting up an Advisory River Board to resolve issues in inter-state cooperation.

The Merchant Shipping Act 1970 aims to deal with waste arising from ships along the coastal areas within a specified radius.

The Water (Prevention and Control of Pollution) Act 1974 establishes an institutional structure for preventing and abating water pollution. It establishes standards for water quality and effluent. Polluting industries must seek permission to discharge waste into effluent bodies. The CPCB (Central Pollution Control Board) was constituted under this act.

1977 - The Water (Prevention and Control of Pollution) Cess Act provides for the levy and collection of 'cess' or 'fees' on water consuming industries and local authorities.

The Water (Prevention and Control of Pollution) Cess Rules 1978 contains the standard definitions and indicate the kind of and location of meters that every consumer of water is required to affix.

The Coastal Regulation Zone Notification 1991 puts regulations on various activities, including construction, are regulated. It gives some protection to the backwaters and estuaries.

Air

The Factories Act and Amendment in 1987 was the first to express concern for the working environment of the workers. The amendment of 1987 has sharpened its environmental focus and expanded its application to hazardous processes.

The Air (Prevention and Control of Pollution) Act 1981 provides for the control and abatement of air pollution. It entrusts the power of enforcing this act to the CPCB.

The Air (Prevention and Control of Pollution) Rules 1982 defines the procedures of the meetings of the Boards and the powers entrusted to them.

The Atomic Energy Act 1982 deals with the radioactive waste.

The Air (Prevention and Control of Pollution) Amendment Act 1987 empowers the central and state pollution control boards to meet with grave emergencies of air pollution.

The Motor Vehicles Act 1988 states that all hazardous waste is to be properly packaged, labelled and transported.

The above laws have been sourced from: Environmental policy-making in India–The process and its pressure, TERI report. Indian Environmental Legislations, list from the MOEF website. Strengthening Environmental Legislations in India, document by Centre for Environmental Law, WWF.

Role of Pollution Control Boards

The nodal agency for implementing various legislations relating to environmental protection at the Centre is the Ministry of Environment and Forest. Besides giving directions to the CPCB on matters relating to prevention and control of pollution, the Ministry of Environment and Forest is responsible for designing and implementing a wide range of programmes relating to environmental protection.

The Central Pollution Control Board (CPCB) was constituted as Central Board for Prevention and Control of Water Pollution (CBPCWP) on 22nd September, 1974 under the provisions of The Water (Prevention & Control of Pollution) Act, 1974, and later under Water (Prevention & Control of Pollution) Amendment Act 1988 (No. 53 of 1988) its name was amended as Central Pollution Control Board.

The CPCB and the SPCBs both are responsible for implementing legislations relating to protection, prevention and control of environmental pollution. Pollution is generated both from point sources, i.e., factories and non-point sources, i.e., automobiles. Source-specific effluent and emission standards have been fixed for polluting point sources. For non-point sources, as monitoring of pollution generation is very difficult, indirect measures of pollution prevention control such as catalytic converters in automobile engine for new cars, led-free petrol, fuel with low sulfur content, periodic inspection of vehicles etc. are being adopted. In addition, ambient standards for air and water have been laid down and are being regularly monitored by the CPCB with the support of the SPCB.

The Central Pollution Control Board has been playing a significant role in controlling environmental pollution by generating and gathering relevant data, providing scientific information, rendering technical inputs for formation of national policies and programmes, training and development of manpower, through activities for promoting awareness at different levels of the Government and Public at large. The Central Board has enlisted the major thrust areas requiring immediate attention and assisted government to formulate National Plans and to execute them appropriately. Government of India recognises the impact of pollution on environment and to ensure that India moves in the right direction, Central Pollution Control Board (CPCB) was established.

The principal function of the Central Pollution Control Board (CPCB) as in 'Water (Prevention and Control of Pollution) Act, 1974' and 'Air (Prevention and Control of Pollution) Act, 1981' are:

- To promote cleanliness of water streams and wells in different areas of the States through prevention, control and abatement of water pollution;
- To improve the quality of air and to prevent, control or abate air pollution in the country;
- Advise and suggest Central Government on any matter concerning prevention and control of water and air pollution and improvement of the air quality;
- Plan and cause to be executed a nation-wide programme for the prevention, control or abatement of water and air pollution;
- Coordinate the activities of the State Boards and resolve disputes among them;

- Provide technical assistance and guidance to the State Boards to carry out and sponsor investigations and research relating to problems of water and air pollution, and for their prevention, control and abatement;
- Plan and organise training to persons who are engaged in programmes for prevention, control or abatement of water and air pollution;
- Organise through mass media, a comprehensive mass awareness programme on prevention, control or abatement of water and air pollution;
- Collect, compile and publish technical and statistical data relating to water and air pollution and the measures devised for their effective prevention, control and abatement;
- Prepare manuals, codes and guidelines relating to treatment and disposal of sewage and trade effluents as well as for stack gas cleaning devises, stacks and ducts;
- Disseminate information in respect of matters relating to water and air pollution and their prevention and control;
- Lay down, modify or annul, in consultation with the State Government concerned, the standards for stream or well, and lay down standards for quality of air;
- Establish or recognize laboratories to enable the Board to perform; and
- Perform such other functions as and when prescribed by the Government of India.
- In addition to the above, the CPCB is empowered, on behalf of the Ministry of Environment and Forests.
- To issue directions to any industry, local bodies, or other authority for violation of the notified general emission and effluent standards, and rules relating to hazardous waste, bio-medical waste, hazardous chemicals, industrial solid waste, municipal solid waste including plastic waste under the Environment (Protection) Rules, 1986.

In the last decade, the environmental awareness towards improving the quality of environment has increased substantially and all efforts are being made at different levels to minimize environmental pollution and thus help in improving the quality of life. Environmental Management means the proper utilisation, conservation, preservation, control and recycling of the natural resources for maintaining a balanced ecosystem. The main focus of environment management is, thus, to avoid the over-use, misuse and abuse of the natural resources.

The effective environmental management is the optimum allocation of finite natural resources among the various possible uses and it has to be based on scientific and technological approach which takes full note of socioeconomic parameters and compulsions.

Environmental management is, thus, an interdisciplinary approach for the conservation of resource and it acts as a regulatory force on human wantonness in resource wasting.

Environmental Movements and Non-Governmental Organisations

In recent years, there has been an increase of governmental interest in environmental problems. The world is widely seen to be in the throes of an environmental problem. As a result, environmental problems have become a serious issue of the political agenda in almost every country. While the degree of popular interest in global environmental degradation may be something novel, the history for the concern about environmental conservation is certainly not new. On the contrary, the origins and early history of contemporary Indian environmental concern and concomitant attempts at conservationist intervention lie far back in time.

The origin of concern for environmental protection in India can be traced back to the early twentieth century when people from different parts in India protested against the commercialisation of forest resources during the British colonial period. In the 1970s a coherent and relatively organised awareness of the ecological impact of state-monolithic development process started to develop to grow into a fully-fledged understanding of the limited nature of natural resources and to prevent the depletion of natural resources.

Environmental movements in India started in the 1970s and 1980s building upon the work of thousands of civil society groups and individuals which were spread across the country. These groups responded to the weaknesses of democratic governance processes in the country. In the subsequent years, environmental movements have gained considerable support both from the media and the judiciary. Its relationship with the political and bureaucratic systems, on the other hand, remains poor and often antagonistic. But given the availability of 'democratic space' within the country, the environmental movement has grown rapidly over the last three to four decades. It has played a key role in three areas:

- in creating public awareness about the importance of bringing about a balance between natural environment and economic development;
- in opposing various development projects that are inimical to social and environmental concerns; and
- in organising model projects that show the way forward towards non-bureaucratic and participatory, community-based natural resource management systems.

India has witnessed a wide range of environmental movements such as Silent Valley Movement in Kerala, Chipko Movement in Uttar Pradesh, Appiko Movement in Karnataka, Bishnoi Movement in Rajasthan, Narmada Bachao Andolan in central India, which aim at halting environmental degradation or bringing about environmental restoration or regeneration or sustainable use of natural resources. Some of them are as:

BISHNOI MOVEMENT

There was a severe drought in a village called Pipasar of Rajasthan in 1471 AD. The drought lasted for three years. Every bit of grass and plants were chopped to feed the animals. Women, children starved, cattle were dying and there was not a single drop of water. People left their homes and migrated in search of water. At that time, there was a man called 'Jambeshwar' who was acutely pained at the tragedy but wisely learnt a lesson. He wisely noticed that, unlike in the past, the land was not able to withstand the destruction from the drought as a large number of trees had been fallen. If life was to survive, people must understand the value of their environment. He preached that the way in which we live should be in complete harmony with nature and not against it. He came to be known as Guru Maharaj Jambaji. Jambaji put down his thoughts into 29 principles which are followed by his disciples who are known as Bishnois (20+9) or twentyniners. According to the religion preached by Jambaji, there was strict ban on:

- Killing of any animal or bird.
- Falling of a green tree.

The unique religion of conservation for environment was taken up by a large number of people in Rajasthan and the number of Bishnois increased to the entire village communities. This helped to make villages greener and restore the natural ecosystems. Vegetation naturally helped to recharge the ground water.

About 300 years after this religion was founded, the soldiers of king of Jodhpur tried to cut trees in a Bishnoi village of Khejadali so that a new palace may be built for the king. The Bishnois tried to reason with them and stop them but in vain. But true of their religion, the Bishnois hugged the trees to protect them. The soldiers attacked them to overcome the protest and 363 Bishnois were killed.

When the king heard of this massacre and the unique religion, he was overcome by people's devotion. He ordered his men to withdraw, gave the religion state sanction and ensured that the wishes of Bishnois were respected in future. Even today, after many

(Picture Depicting: Bishnoi Movement for tree protection)

generations, Bishnois continue to protect the trees and animals. One can spot a Bishnoi village easily as being greener and more abundant in wildlife. The population of Black Buck, which is in the list of endangered species, is found to be in great number in Bishnoi villages than outside. In today's environment, when many places are facing acute shortage of water and pollution of air, land and water, we need to take a lesson from Bishnois. Conservation is a religion every human being should adopt.

CHIPKO MOVEMENT

The word chipko means to stick to or to hug and refers to the method used to protect the trees of the Himalaya from commercial timber cutters who have devastated the forests. The movement's activists embrace the tree trunks to interpose their bodies between the trees and the axemen. The Chipko movement is located in the mountainous northern segment of Uttar Pradesh, immediately west of Nepal. The area has long been known as Uttarakhand, a term recently revived by persons seeking self-government and perhaps statehood for the region. Persons with this political motive are few in number and are primarily members of the urban elite. In contrast, the members of the environmental movement are chiefly indigenous subsistence farmers, both Indo-Aryan-speaking Hindus of the lower Himalaya who are called Pahari and, in fewer numbers, Tibetan-speaking Buddhists of the higher Himalaya who are known as Bhotiya.

In the 1970s, an organised resistance to the destruction of forests spread throughout India and came to be known as the Chipko movement. The name of the movement comes from the word 'embrace', as the villagers hugged the trees, and prevented the contractors from falling them.

Not many people know that over the last few centuries many communities in India have helped save nature. One such is the Bishnoi community of Rajasthan. The original 'Chipko movement' was started around 260 years back in the early part of the 18th century in Rajasthan by this community. A large group of them from 84 villages led by a lady called Amrita Devi laid down their lives in an effort to protect the trees from being fallen on the orders of the *Maharaja* (King) of

Jodhpur. After this incident, the *maharaja* gave a strong royal decree preventing the cutting of trees in all Bishnoi villages.

During the 20th century, it started in the hills where the forests are the principal source of livelihood, since agricultural activities cannot be carried out easily. The Chipko movement 1973 was one of the most famous among these environmental movements. The first Chipko action took place spontaneously in April 1973 in the Mandal village of the upper Alakananda valley and over the next five years spread to many districts of the Himalayas in Uttar Pradesh. It was sparked off by the government's decision to allot a plot of forest area in the Alaknanda valley to a sports goods company. This angered the surrounding villagers because their similar demand to use wood for making agricultural tools had been denied earlier. With encouragement from a local NGO, DGSS (Dasoli Gram Swarajya Sangh), the women of the area, under the leadership of a social activist, Chandi Prasad Bhatt, went into the forest and formed a circle around the trees preventing the men from cutting them down.

The success achieved by this protest led to similar environmental protests in other regions of the country. From their origins as a spontaneous protest against logging abuses in Uttar Pradesh in the Himalayas, supporters of the Chipko movement, mainly women from villages, have successfully banned the felling of trees in a number of regions and influenced natural resource policy in India. Dhoom Singh Negi, Bachni Devi and many other village women, were the first to save trees by hugging them. They coined a slogan: *'What do the Forests bear? Soil, Water and Pure Air'*.

The success of the Chipko movement in the hills saved thousands of trees from being fallen.

Many other people have also been involved in this movement and have given it an appropriate direction. Mr. Sunderlal Bahuguna, a Gandhian activist and philosopher, whose appeal to Mrs. Indira Gandhi, the then Prime Minister of India, resulted in the green tree falling ban. Mr. Bahuguna coined the Chipko slogan: *'Ecology is permanent economy'*. Mr. Chandi Prasad Bhatt, is another prominent leader of the Chipko movement. He pioneered and encouraged the development of local industries based on the conservation and sustainable use of forest wealth for local benefit. Mr. Ghanshyam Raturi, the Chipko poet, whose songs echo throughout the Himalayas of Uttar Pradesh, wrote a poem describing the method of embracing the trees to save them from being fallen: *' Embrace the trees and Save them from being fallen; The property of our hills, save them from being looted.'*

The Chipko protests in Uttar Pradesh achieved a significant victory in 1980 with a 15-year ban on green falling in the Himalayan forests of that state by the order of Mrs. Indira Gandhi, the then Prime Minister of India. Since then, the movement has spread in various states in the country. In addition to the 15-year ban in Uttar Pradesh, the movement has stopped falling in the Western Ghats and the Vindhyas and has generated pressure for a natural resource policy that is more sensitive to people's needs and ecological requirements.

APPIKO MOVEMENT

In Karnataka state, the Appiko movement began in September 1983, when 163 men, women, and children hugged the trees and forced the lumberjacks to leave. That movement swiftly spread to the adjoining districts. These people are against the kind of commercial felling of trees which clears the vegetation in its entirety. They do recognize the firewood needs of urban people (mostly poor) and therefore do not want a total ban on felling. However, they are against indiscriminate cutting and would like to see a consultative process established so that local people are able to participate in timber management.

In Karnataka, Chipko movement is locally known as *Appiko Chaluvali*, was successful in saving trees from falling. Similar successes were achieved in the forests of Bengaon, Husre, and Nidgod. All these grass-root efforts to stop falling led to a policy change within the Indian government that was more focused on the requirements of people and ecological impact.

Uttar Kannada is a densely forested district in the state of Karnataka in the western part of the country. The district is unique in a way that it traverses five important terrestrial eco-zones. From the west to the east there is the narrow coastal plain, the evergreen and

moist deciduous forests of the Western Ghats, the dry deciduous forests and further east the scrublands, making it one of the important centers of biodiversity in the Western Ghats. People have traditionally been involved in social forestry, agro forestry and have maintained unique multi-tiered spice orchards dominated by betel nut (*Areca catechu*).

Movement to save forest

With the falling and commercialisation of this natural forest, the Appiko movement rose: a popular people's response against deforestation and the ruin of ancient livelihoods. At the same time the forest department was involved in clearing of natural ever green forest and plantation of monoculture of Teak and Eucalyptus. This destruction of tropical natural forests and the raising of monoculture plantations of Teak and Eucalyptus caused irreversible changes in the forest ecosystem. The destruction of mixed species denied people access to biomass for fodder, fertilisers, etc.

The clear felling of natural forests has led to severe erosion of soil and drying up of perennial water resources. Moved by the destruction of essential ecological processes, the youth of Salkani village in Sirsi launched an environmental movement called Chipko movement which was locally known as 'Appiko Chaluvali'. They embraced the trees to be felled by contractors of the forest department. The protest within the forest continued for thirty-eight days and finally the felling orders were withdrawn. The success of this protest spread to various other places and the movement has now been launched in eight areas covering the entire Sirsi forest division in Uttara Kannada and Shimoga districts. These areas included Mathghatta, Salkani, Balegadde, Husei, Nedgod, Kelgin Jaddi, Vanalli and Andagi, the rapid spread of the movement was based on evidence provided by villagers that the forest department was over-exploiting the forests. Appiko Andolan gave birth to a new awareness all over southern India.

The Appiko Movement aims to save the remaining forests in the Western Ghats through organising decentralised groups at the grassroots level to take direct action. All these objectives are implemented through locally established Parisara Samrakshna Kendras (environmental conservation centers).

Appiko has neither been opposed to growth nor development. It views nature conservation as complementary to human growth and survival. While forests are destroyed for monetary returns, it must be remembered that there is no way of replacing the fundamental role of tropical forests in pulling the strong oceanic currents to offload their showers. As the threat of climate change becomes real, there cannot be anything more urgent and important than protecting the monsoon gateway of the country, i.e. the Sahyadri range.

NARMADA BACHAO ANDOLAN

Narmada Bachao Andolan is the most powerful mass movement, which was started in 1985 against the construction of a big dam on the river NarmadaHYPERLINK "http://www.ecoindia.com/rivers/narmada.html". The Narmada river is the IndiaHYPERLINK "http://www.ecoindia.com/rivers/narmada.html"'HYPERLINK "http://www.ecoindia.com/rivers/narmada.html"s largest west flowing river, which supports and nurtures a large number of people of various culture and tradition ranging from the indigenous people inhabited in the jungles here to the large number of rural population. However, the proposed Sardar Sarovar Dam and Narmada Sagar have the capacity to displace more than 250,000 people. The ongoing big fight is over the resettlement or the rehabilitation of these people. It is a multi-crore project that will generate large amount of revenue for the Indian government. The Narmada Valley Development Plan is the most prominent and most challenging project in Indian history. The proponents are of the view that it will produce more than 1450 MW of electricity and also provide drinking water to over 40 million people covering thousands of villages and towns. Some of the dams have already been constructed like, Tawa and Bargi Dams. But the opponents argue that this hydro project will devastate human lives and bio diversity by affecting thousands of acres of forests and main agricultural land. On the other hand, it will overall displace and deprive thousands of people of their livelihood. They believe that the water and energy could be provided to the people through alternative technological means that would be ecologically beneficial.

Narmada Bachao Aandolan

This movement was led by one of the prominent leaders Medha Patkar. It has now been turned into the International protest, gaining world wide support from NGOHYPERLINK "http://www.ecoindia.com/rivers/narmada.html"'HYPERLINK http://www.ecoindia.com/rivers/narmada.htmls all over the world. Protestors are agitating the issue through the mass media, hunger strikes, massive marches, rallies and the through the screening of several documentary films. HYPERLINK "http://www.ecoindia.com/rivers/narmada.html"Although they have been protesting peacefully, but they been harassed, arrested and beaten up by the police several times. The Narmada Bachao Andolan is also pressurising the world-bank to withdraw its loan from the project through media.

SILENT VALLEY MOVEMENT

Save Silent ValleyHYPERLINK "http://www.ecoindia.com/rivers/narmada.html" was a social movement aimed at the protection of Silent valley, an evergreen tropical forest in the Palakkad district of Kerala, India. It was started in 1973 to save the HYPERLINK "http://en.wikipedia.org/wiki/Silent_Valley_National_Park"Silent Valley Reserve Foresting from being flooded by a hydroelectric project. The valley was declared as Silent Valley National Park in 1985.

Silent Valley movement is concerned with the proposed construction of a river valley project to fetch the need of electricity and irrigation to the people around that particular area. Since early, this project was started; it was opposed by various NGOs and environmentalists as it could cause serious damage to this 'cradle of evolution'- the home to numerous rare and important species of plants and animals.

The Silent Valley is one of the few remaining undisturbed rain-forest areas in India which lies in the Malabar region, the least developed section of the state of Kerala in the Western Ghats. Located in remote area from main urban centers or highways, the valley has experienced relatively little timber cutting and almost none of the peasant or tribal farming that characterises the rest of rural southern India. Various rare species of plants, ferns, and endangered fauna survive in this valley. During the early 1960s the state government started planning a dam for the Kuntipuzha River, which flows through the valley to generate hydroelectricity as the basis for regional economic development. The project offers a classic example of the dilemma between natural environment and economic development.

Dam Construction

The Kerala People's Science Movement is a network of rural school teachers and local citizens that preserves and promotes environmental scientific projects in the villages. The movement recognised the obvious economic needs of the people of Malabar but concluded that the Silent Valley project would make only a small contribution to regional development. Thus the groups opposed the project with a campaign that brought into sharp focus on the ecological consequences, specifically the possibility of extinction of the rare species that had evolved over millions of years. Villagers in Kerala also learned that establishment of new industries and clear cutting of timber in the upper watersheds of the river were contributing to the disruption of streams and water supplies.

The movement was started to challenge the idea that energy generated by the dam would benefit the rural people of Kerala. Most of the energy from the project was to be exported to industrialised areas of Kerala and surrounding states. The movement asserted that the local environment would be severely disrupted with benefits going to Trivandrum, the state capital.

The state government favoured the project, but other environmental groups expressed doubts. After years of activism the movement persuaded the Indian government to appoint a high-level committee to examine the project's environmental and socioeconomic effects. The committee subsequently recommended abandonment of the scheme, which the state government accepted in 1983. The controversy over the Silent Valley project marked the fiercest environmental dispute in India and established a precedent wherever a major development project, specifically a dam, threatened ecological balance. For example, Save the Narmada Movement cited the decision about the Silent Valley in mobilising support for its stance against dam projects.

BALIYAPAL MOVEMENT

When in 1985, the government of India decided to construct a test base for missiles in the area of Baliapal in north Odisha, on India's Bay of Bengal coast its purpose was to research, produce, and launch missiles and satellites. Baliapal place was chosen as the strategic location for a variety of military reasons, among them its distance from major population centers, air and sea routes, and Pakistani radar surveillance; its lack of oil and mineral deposits; and its cyclone-free weather but the establishment of the missile base necessitated the eviction of more than 100,000 peasant farmers and fisher folk from their homes and lands. In response to the threat of eviction and the destruction of their livelihoods, the people of Baliapal established a nonviolent social movement, 50,000 persons strong, to resist the government.

Resistance by the local Baliapal population to the missile base was motivated by both economic and cultural factors that were specific to the Baliapal area. These factors informed the Baliapal movement's identity and ideology and were relayed through a poetics of resistance that included songs, dramas, and symbols. Under the title MahaRakhyasaKhepanastra (Great secret resistance), more than sixty-five songs about the Baliapal movement and the local culture were written by a paan (betel leaf) trader, Purushottam Behera, one of the leaders of the movement.

The songs celebrated the agricultural richness and diversity of Baliapal and the prosperity it had brought to the peasants. They articulated those commonly held feelings that comprised a Baliapali's sense of place. They also evoked Hindu folklore and believe in an attempt to provide religious and moral credence to the Baliapalis' claim to the land.

The movement's identity and ideology drew upon the cultural and economic dimensions of the peasants' everyday reality. It converted the cultural sentiment for the land - the peasant's sense of place - into a political demand for the absolute right to its continued use through religious and mythical tools. The Government could not implement its decision because of the strong resistance of the people.

THE PLCHIMADA STRUGGLE

> *"It is a new experience for us that water becomes a market commodity. It is alien to our habits. To sell bottled water is unjust and anti-nature."*

Veloor Swaminathan describes the rationale of this struggle in these above simple statements. This struggle was started against the multi-national Coca-Cola factory at Plachimada of Perumatty Panchayat in Chittoor Taluk of Palakkad district, Kerala. It has shown great consistency and perseverance in the recent years. It has attracted significant amount of international media attention and thus it is being projected as a role model of resistance against multi-national colonisation. As a result, similar struggles against Coca-Cola and the over exploitation of scarce groundwater resources for its sake, is getting attention in Sivaganga in Tamil Nadu and in the state of Odisha. All these struggles have to be reviewed in a perspective that would unveil the exploitative face of globalisation and its agents, the multi-national giants. Rugmini (46), a resident of Plachimada area, says that she does not experience any water scarcity before the company started functioning.

> *"We live here for the last 20 years. Before two years we need not have to go out to fetch water. But today we walk a distance of two and a half kilometers to collect two pots of water. The Panchayat who is supposed to serve the people do not take any action to resolve this problem".*

The people of this region are agitating against the human rights violation of the factory for many years. People representing the five most affected colonies adjacent to the established factory, who belong to Eravala, Malasar tribal communities and other scheduled caste communities have been holding demonstrations and sitting for strike in front of the factory for many years. On April 22nd, 2002, around 2000 men, women and children dwelling around the Hindustan Coca-Cola Beverages Pvt. Ltd at Plachimada, picketed the factory and gave an ultimatum to the authorities to quit immediately. The Adivasi Gotrasabha leader Ms. C.K. Janu initiated the overwhelming function. The police, however, arrested all the people participated in the function. Blockades, Dharna and Picketing were all resorted to during this ongoing protest against the wrongs of factory by the poor and weak people.

The police blaming them of raising slogans against the multinational company, stopping the workers from going to the factory and indulging in various anti-social activities, registered several cases against these poor people and their leaders. The company filed a petition in the High Court demanding police protection from these 'anti-social elements'. The accused were Vilayodi Venugopal who is Chairman of Adivasi Protection Council and Veloor Swaminathan the Convenor of Action Council, Subrahmanyan, Murukesan, Kochikkadu Mani, and Pazhaniswmi. However, the High Court also accepted a counter petition file submitted by the Action Council explaining that they were waging a very just protest and it was their legitimate and valid right to demonstrate in a peaceful and democratic manner. The MNC, however, was smart enough to influence the media not to give coverage to the struggle.

However, the newspapers except a few and cannot go against the wishes and interests of the MNCs like the HCC. Political parties, irrespective of their political ideologies for or against globalisation and WTO, have wooed their best to protect the interests of the factory depriving the basic human rights and physical existence of those who elected them to power. As the days went by the national media just cannot but to give due coverage as the struggle was gaining high momentum and international media attention, cases were registered one after another but it did not affect the morale or political will of the people whatever be the financial burden it rendered. The giant factory that can literally dictate terms to political rulers, law enforcement agencies, civil servants etc., used its money power and muscle power to silence the people and it has been partly successful so much so that the police department, despite the fact that the petition by the factory for Police protection was dismissed by the high court of Kerala, has misinformed the people that the factory has been granted police protection by the high court. There is heavy deployment of police at the gate of the factory threatening the poor people of dire consequences if any attempt is made against the smooth functioning of the factory.

Non Governmental Organisations

Non-governmental organisations have emerged as prominent players to perform various types of tasks. They help in designing and implementing environment policies, programmes and action plans, set out specifications. For EIAs, they play significant roles through their environmental campaigns, educate the public about the environment campaigns, educate the public about the environment and raise awareness among them.

NGOs have, in particular, played significant role in raising issues related to environmental concerns, developing awareness of environmental issues and promoting sustainable development. The encouragement of public participation in environmental management through legislation in recent years has also enhanced the role of NGOs and Major Groups. They also question the wrong policies of any government, marshalling public opinion and even guide them in formulating policies.

In some countries, community participation is required by law for implementation of policies and plans, where NGOs play the dominant role in liaising with the stakeholders-the government and the people.

Even some movements, like the Chipko movement which started in a district of the Himalayas, by a group of tribal women to resist tree felling and the Narmada Bachao Andolan has raised its voice in environment development issues and have mobilised masses into action. Some novel concepts like people's tribunals which look after the cases filed by individuals or communities affected by environmental degradation have also been adopted.

Some organisations have helped the local people, by providing them trade contacts who wish to manage their resources in an efficient and sustainable way and some others have helped the local populace by ecotourism. As the local people know more about their forests, they have been employed as guides, trackers etc.

Some NGOs are small and work in a particular small and specific area. For example, Wildlife First! a small NGO that works on eco-development projects around the Bhadra National Park. Some of them are very big and work worldwide. For example, the World Wildlife Fund for Nature (WWF) is a large organisation, working in quite a large number of countries. Some NGOs form a consortium of many organisations and work towards achieving a common goal.

Participation of community has long been known to be a prerequisite for the success of any project. Moreover, as custodians of the wealth that they have been endowed with, the local people have more at stake than any others to protect and judiciously use of environment.

In recent years, the number of activities undertaken by environmental NGOs and other major voluntary groups has broadened. They now undertake a much wider range of activities than simply raising environmental awareness and acting as pressure groups. Their activities now comprise environmental monitoring, promoting environmental education, training and capacity-building, implementing demonstration projects, conducting advocacy work in partnership with the government, and the promotion of regional and international cooperation on environment. Many also get involved in the practical management of conservation areas, and promote community or individual action and campaign for greater accountability on the part of the government and corporate sector.

A number of NGOs in the region now work sincerely on environment and development, thus acknowledging that environmental problems are embedded in unnatural use of natural resources for economic and social systems. The conviction that NGOs and government agencies can and should work together in a complementary relationship has become stronger and the credibility that NGOs have acquired from successful campaigns has created strong and growing public support for their new advocacies.

There has been several Non-Governmental Organisations that are working properly towards environmental protection in our country. They have, however, led to growing interest in environmental protection and conservation of nature and natural resources. The traditional conservation practices, which were part of ancient India's culture, have, however, gradually disappeared. Public awareness is thus a vital need to future environmental protection.

The Bombay Natural History Society (BNHS), Mumbai: The BNHS was started as a small society of six members in 1883. It grew up from a group of *shikaris* and people from all walks of life into an important research organisation that substantially influences conservation policy in the country. Its major influence on wildlife policy building, research, popular publications and peoples' action has been a unique feature of the multifaceted society. It is India's oldest conservation research-based NGO and one that has been at the forefront of the battle for preservation and conservation of species and ecosystems.

World Wide Fund for Nature-India (WWF-I), New Delhi: The WWF-I was established in 1969 in Mumbai and later on the headquarters were shifted to Delhi with several branch offices all over India. During the early years, focused of attention were to wildlife education and generation of awareness. It runs several programmes, including the Nature Clubs of India programme for school children and works as a think tank and lobby force for environmental and developmental issues.

Kalpvriksh, Pune: This NGO, initially Delhi-based, is now working from Pune and is active in several other parts of India. Kalpvriksh works on a variety of fronts: education and awareness; investigation and research; direct action and lobbying; and litigation with regard to environment and development issues. It is involved in the preparation of site-specific environmental manuals for school teachers. Kalpvriksh was among those responsible for developing India's National Biodiversity Strategy and Action Plan in 2003.

The NGOs are facilitators, educators, defenders and are very important in helping the people and their environment. Some of the important Indian NGOs are the following:

1. The Energy Resources Institute, Delhi.
2. Bombay Natural History Society, Maharashtra.
3. Institute of Advance Study in Science and Technology, Assam.
4. Indian Centre for Plastic in the Environment, Maharashtra.
5. Environment Management Division-Confederation of Indian Industries, Delhi.
6. Development Alternatives, Delhi.
7. World Wide Fund for Nature-India (WWF), Delhi.
8. Centre for Environment Education (CEE), Gujarat.
9. Environment Protection Training and Research Institute, Andhra Pradesh.
10. Indian Environmental Society, Delhi.
11. Centre for Media Studies, Delhi.
12. Centre for Symbiosis of Technology, Delhi.
13. Consumer Education and Research Centre, Gujarat.
14. CPR Environmental Education Centre, Tamil Nadu.

15. Foundation for Revitalisation of Local Health Traditions, Karnataka.
16. National Solid Waste Association of India (NSWAI), Maharashtra.
17. Sulabh International Institute of Health and Hygiene, Delhi.
18. Waterfalls Institute of Technology Transfer (WITT), Delhi.
19. Salim Ali Centre for Ornithology and Natural History (SACON), Tamil Nadu.
20. Environmental Management and Policy Research Institute (EMPRI), Karnataka.
21. International Institute for Population Sciences (IIPS), Maharashtra.

Local, regional and national NGOs have emerged as major players and partners in both development and conservation activities in the region.

At the community level, they are in the front line in providing assistance in the acquisition of basic needs and amenities; in identifying issues, raising awareness, and providing information to grassroots communities; in articulating the communities' problems and needs and bringing these to the attention of those who can affect change; in defending both the environmental and developmental rights of communities and building the capacity of communities to manage their natural resources; and in dealing with sustainable development concerns.

NGOs, who work at the national level, focus mainly on policy work and play a vital role in the identification of the weaknesses and gaps in ongoing policy or legal frameworks and in information gathering and educating the public, private sector and government; and, in certain cases, they act as lobby and conduct protest movements.

It has been seen that in recent year mankind's consciousness has been aroused very strongly towards environmental protection and ecological preservation. It is of vital importance that the people should be aware not only of the problems involved but also of the role to be played in protecting the environment. Along with the people's participation at each level, the formal education and awareness programmed should be provided and implementing various environmental protection projects. In addition, it is also very essential to develop environment friendly technologies and renewable energy sources following the principle of conservation.

While developing technologies are used for the benefit of man, it is also essential to study their adverse impact on the natural environment so that cyclic processes, which the nature has devised for conservation of resources is not affected badly. Air, water and land are the basic amenities of human life. But with the increasing over population and growing rapid industrialisation has created a state of decadence in the natural environment man has continuously tampered with the nature. As a result, a danger of threat to his life has been increased due to the lack of healthy fresh air and potable drinking water and the imbalance established in the biosphere.

It is established fact that Earth is the only planet endowed with an environment and we all share it. One day we would pass it on to our future generation as their legacy. But if they will inherit such a polluted environment, life will be misery for them. Man has improved the technologies and other means which are necessary for higher production of wealth and exploited nature for his benefits, but without any foresight as to what the implications of his actions would be on the environment. Rapid growing of industrialisation has resulted in urban migration from rural areas and consequently it has led to slum development, which in turn resulted in the pollution of environment.

Before the advent of modern civilisation man lived and flourished amidst the nice balance of natural environment. As the most intelligent being on earth man has constantly tampered the nature making use of his inventive genius and disturbed the ecological balance. Thus, air, water and soil, all have got polluted and posing threat to the substance of mankind. The result will be in numerous health problems. Air pollution has become a severe problem today which is the direct implication of industrialisation and urbanisation. The chimneys of factories emit smoke and vehicles emit fumes, which directly have contributed to air pollution. Any gaseous material which constitute excess of sulphur dioxide, carbon monoxide, nitrogen dioxide, dust etc. in air cause air pollution. Air pollution also occurs when there is forest-fire, rubber plants are gutted or plastics are burnt along with the household garbage. This kind of pollution has been aggravated more today because of atomic explosions in some developed countries. The hovering over some cities in the early morning is also the result of air pollution. The depletion of ozone layer is also due to air pollution and it may result in skin diseases.

The emission of greenhouse (GHGs) like carbon dioxide, CFCs, methane, in increased concentration has led to climate changes. These gases are responsible for green-house effect and thus for global warming.

Most of the air pollutants directly affect the respiratory and cardiovascular systems. Nitrogen dioxide and ozone also effect the respiratory system, irritate the eyes, nose and throat and in addition ozone can cause headaches. Carbon monoxide is able to displace oxygen in the blood which in turn can result in cardiovascular and neurological effects. Lead affects bone narrow, impairs liver and kidney function, causes neurological damage and limits metal development in children. Mercury causes *minimata* disease.

Although earth is surrounded by water in its three-fourth areas, yet drinking water has a scarcity. All main source of portable water like rivers, lakes, ponds, even wells have been polluted by various dangerous chemical and biological wastes. The congeal mixture of dirt, sewage and industrial waste has polluted the river water severely on whose bank the factories are established. Increased use of chemical fertilisers and insecticides also pollutes the drinking water of river, ponds and wells. The harmful fertilisers and insecticides even seep through the earth and pollute the ground water. The polluted water supply results in epidemic like cholera, jaundice and gastroenteritis etc.

Soil is being polluted in numerous ways. Soil pollution is the results of the disposal of solid and semisolid wastes from agricultural practices and unsanitary habits. Excessive use of harmful pesticides and chemical fertilisers are resulting in both biological and chemical contamination. Rapid rate of growing industrialisation and urbanisation has disposed enormous solid and semisolid wastes at different places polluting soil, air as well as water. Apart from these pathogenic organisms also pose threat to land pollution. Thus, soil is getting severely polluted day by day by hazardous materials and micro-organisms which enter food chain or water and are consequently ingested by man. As a result, there are various health problems like dysentery, cholera and paratyphoid fever. However, increased use of plastics, polythene and other non-degradable products has led to the problem of their disposal.

We are facing numerous kinds of problems today. These are like air pollution, water pollution, soil pollution and noise pollution etc. Noise pollution is due to the unbearable sound being produced by frequent playing of loud speakers, radios and televisions, ceaseless loud sound of vehicles deafens us in day time. Research has been showing that noise pollution is capable of causing ulcers, abortions, cardiovascular diseases, sleeplessness and hypertension besides several mental disorders.

Food pollution is another problem we have been facing today. We suffer from several diseases because of the polluted food items that we take. After the advent of nuclear weapons, the exposure level of ionizing radiations has been increased which is hazardous to people. The ill-effects due to radioactive pollution are cancers, genetic damage and mutations leading to abnormal birth.

Protection of environmental pollution is the need of hour. If it is not checked properly, the earth will become a graveyard. So, we must give due attention to protect it from human's bad practices. We must have balanced and planned industrial growth in order to check this pollution. Towns and cities should be planned carefully and proper attention should be given on plantation of more trees.

There are a lot to be done immediately to make the area polluted free one. As the present status of the movement seems to be inconsistent and unorganised, to make the area polluted free becomes a mirage.

Keeping up continuous people's participation, vigilance, pressure on politicians and government machinery and the industry is the only way to protect the environment and attain sustainable development. The community should rise to the occasion and make its voice heard against such disasters. No industry should be allowed into any locality or village without a complete presentation to the community of what its activities would entail. In like manner, there is space for environmental NGOs, social and environmental activists, media etc. in highlighting the environmental problems and mobilising people to find solutions for the problem. More studies are necessary for evolving suitable methodologies both for protection of the environment and for continuous participation of the people as a watchdog against pollution.

References

1. Agrawal, Anil and Sunita Naraiyan. 1985. *The State of India's Environment, 1984-85: The Second Citizen Report*. New Delhi: Centre For Science and Environment.
2. Bharucha, Erach. 2003. *Biodiversity of India*. The Mapin Publishing.
3. Bharucha, Erach. 2005. *Environmental Studies*. University Press.
4. Centre for Science and Environment (1983), *State of Environment in India: The Second Citizen Report*, New Delhi.
5. Centre for Science and Environment. *Down to Earth* (various issues), New Delhi.
6. Chand, Attar. 1985. *Environmental Challenges: A Global Survey.* Delhi: UBH Publishers.
7. De, A.K. 2000. *Environmental Chemistry*. New Age International.
8. Dwivedi, O.P & Dhirendra K. Bajpayi (eds). 1995. *Environmental Policies in Third World: A Comparative Analysis*. Westport: Greenwood Press.
9. Dwivedi, O.P. 1997. *India's Environmental Policies, Programmes and Stewardship*. Macmillan, New Delhi.
10. Gautam, A. & R. Rastogi. 2001. *Geography of India*. Meerut: International Publication House.
11. Government of India (Ministry of Environment & Forests), 1992. *Policy Statement for Abatement of Pollution*, New Delhi.
12. Gregory, D. 1985. *The Geographical Imagination, Social Theory and Human Geography*. London: Hutchinson.
13. Gupta, S., 1996. 'Environmental Policy and Federalism in India', National Institute of Public Finance and Policy, New Delhi.
14. Helmut Fleischer. 1973. *Marxism and History*. New York: Harper Torchbooks.
15. https://www.britannica.com/science/global-warming
16. https://www.cbd.int/doc/press/2021/pr-2021-03-24-brazil-en.pdf
17. Hudson N. (1995). *Soil Conservation*. London: B. T. Batsford Limited.
18. Husain, M (ed.). 1994. *Sustainable Development and Environmental Impact Assessment: Sustainable Development.* New Delhi.
19. Hussain, M. 2002. *Human Geography*. Rawat Publications, Jaipur.

20. Hussain, M. 2004. *Evolution of Geographical Thought, 5th ed.* Jaipur: Rawat Publications.

21. Jadhav, H & V.M. Bhosale. *Environment Protection and Laws*. Himalaya Publishing House.

22. Kothari, A. 1993. *Conservation of Biological Diversity in India*. New Delhi:Indian Institute of Public Administration.

23. Kumar, R. 1987. *Environmental Pollution and Health Hazards in India*. New Delhi: Ashish Publishing House.

24. Mahesh Rangarajan (ed.). 2006. *Environmental Issues in India: A Reader*. New Delhi.

25. Maurya, S.D (ed.). 1989. *Urbanisation and Environmental Problems*. Allahabad: Chugh Publications.

26. Mehta, S., S. Mundle and U. Sankar, 1993/1997. *Controlling Pollution: Incentives and Regulation,* Sage, New Delhi.

27. Miller, T.G 1999. *Environmental Science*. Wadsworth Publishing.

28. Ministry of Power, Government of India 2010 (www.powermin.nic.in).

29. Rangarajan, Mahesh. 2001. *India's Wildlife History*. Permanent Black Publications.

30. Roy Choudhury, S.P. 1989. *Land and Soil*. New Delhi: NBT.

31. Sahu, Nirmal Chand *et al*. *Dimensions of Environmental and Ecological Economics*. Universities Press.

32. Singh, R.B and S. Mishra (eds). 1996. *Environmental Law in India Issues and Responses*. New Delhi: Concept Publishing House.

33. Singh, Savindra. 2009. *Physical Geography.* Prayag Pustak Bhawan, Allahabad.

34. The Indian Express, 09 August 2021.

35. The Hindu, August 02, 2020.

36. The Hindu, 10 August 2021

37. Tiwari, R. C. 1993. *Geography of India*. New Delhi: Tata McGraw Hill.

38. Tiwari, R.C. 2006. *Geography of India*. Prayag Pustak Bhawan, Allahabad.

39. Valdiya, K.S. 2004. *Geology, Environment and Society*. University Press.

40. Valdiya, K.S. *Coping with Natural Hazards: Indian Context*. Orient Blackswan.

41. Wadia, D. N. 1993. *Geology of India*. New Delhi: NBT.

42. World Bank. 1992. *Development and the Environment*, World Bank.

43. World Commission on Environment and Development. 1987. *Our Common Future*. Oxford: Oxford University Press.

44. World Development Report. 1992. *Development and the Environment.* New York: Oxford University Press.

Glossary

Environment- is the surrounding of atmosphere which influences development or growth of people, animal or plants, living or working conditions.

Biotic- is the living components of planet earth.

Abiotic-is the non-living components of planet earth.

Ecology - is the study of the interrelationships of living organisms and, especially, of groups of living organisms among themselves and between them and the non-living (or physical) environment.

Ecological approach- emphasizes on the relation between the organism and its environment and the relation between perception and action.

Economic determinism- is the theory which gives primacy to the economic structure over politics in the development of human history.

Possibilistic approach- is a philosophy which attempts to explain man and environment relationship in a different way, taking man as an active agent in environment.

Teleological approach- is, in literal terms, the study of purposes, goals, or ends.

Determinism approach – emphasizes on the view that landscapes are mainly determined by the environment.

Environmental pollution – can be understood as any undesirable change in physical, chemical and biological characteristics of our air, land and water.

Air pollution – depicts the accumulation of harmful gases in the atmosphere that endanger human health or produce other measured effects on living matter and other materials.

Water pollution – describes, any physical, biological or chemical change in water quality that adversely affects living organisms or makes water unsuitable for their use.

Land pollution – is the degradation of the Earth's land surface through the faulty use of the soil by faulty agricultural practices, mineral exploitation, industrial waste dumping, and indiscriminate disposal of urban wastes.

Noise pollution – is an accumulation and composite of sounds generated by human activities ranging from blasting stereo systems to the roar of ballistic missile and supersonic transport jets.

Solar pond – is a large body of water for the collection and storage of solar energy.

Geothermal energy – is used to indicate that part of the Earth's heat contained within the Earth that generates geological phenomena on a planetary scale.

Sustainable development – is the development that fulfils the needs of the present without compromising the quality for future generations to meet their own needs.

Agenda 21- is a blueprint for environment and development into the 21st century.

Environmental Planning – is said to be a facilitating decision process and to carry out development with due consideration given to the natural environmental social, political, economic and governance factors and provides overall frame work to achieve sustainable outcomes.

Afforestation- is plantation of trees on large scale.

Agroforestry- Where tree and field crops are grown together in the same field.

Land Degradation- The deterioration of land through such processes as soil erosion, salinisation, acidification, pollution, or sediment deposition.

Soil Conservation- The combinations of appropriate land use and management practices that promote the productive and sustainable use of soils and in the process minimize soil erosion and other forms of land degradation.

Soil Erosion- is the wearing away of the soil by water, wind, ice, or other geological agents.

Environmental protection- is a method of protecting the environment for the development and benefit of the natural environment and human society.

National Environment Policy- is the central objective to our government for a clean environment, which is mandated in the Constitution in Articles 48 A and 51 A (g). It emphasizes that maintaining a healthy environment is not only the responsibility of the state alone, but to that of every citizen.

Environmental movement- is a social movement which aims at protecting our environment against unsustainable use.

Chipko Movement– refers to the method of protecting trees of the Himalaya from commercial timber cutters who have led the forest to be devastated. The movement's activists embrace the tree and interpose their bodies between the trees and the tree cutters.

Pollution- any undesirable change in atmosphere which is non-suitable to living in it.

Central Pollution Control Board (CPCB)- is the central body of monitoring the pollution which was constituted on 22nd September, 1974 under the provisions of The Water (Prevention & Control of Pollution) Act, 1974. It was later under Water (Prevention & Control of Pollution) Amendment Act 1988, its name was amended as Central Pollution Control Board (CPCB). The CPCB and the SPCBs both are responsible for planning and implementing legislations relating to prevention and control of pollution.

Narmada Bachao Andolan- is a powerful mass movement, which was started in 1985 against the construction of dam on the Narmada River.

Non-Governmental Organisation- is a legally constituted organisation created by natural or legal persons that operates independently from any form of government.

Index

B

C

D

E

F

H

I

J

K

N

O

P

Q

R

S

T

Y

Z